KT-143-123

Huile d'olive

Terence and Vicki Conran

CLASSIC CONRAN

Plain, simple and satisfying food

Photography by Georgia Glynn Smith

TED SMART

above: Roast Beef with Roast Potatoes
page 2: Sardines on Toast

First published in 2003
by Conran Octopus Limited,
a part of Octopus Publishing Group,
2–4 Heron Quays, London E14 4JP
www.conran-octopus.co.uk

This edition produced for
The Book People Ltd, Hall Wood Avenue,
Haydock, St Helens, WA11 9UL

Publishing Director: Lorraine Dickey
Senior Editor: Katey Day
Creative Director: Leslie Harrington
Designer: Victoria Burley
Photography: Georgia Glynn Smith
Senior Production Controller: Manjit Sihra

British Cataloguing-in-Publication Data.
A catalogue record for this book is available from the British Library
ISBN 1 84091 354 1
Printed and bound in China

All recipes serve 4 unless otherwise stated.

CONTENTS

Introduction

We wrote *Classic Conran* because we greatly enjoy the pleasures of preparing, cooking and eating plain and simple food. That is, food which is good and nutritious, flavoursome and seasonal, uncomplicated and uncluttered, where the quality of the ingredients is paramount and where the time spent making the dishes is usually short. This book is a collection of the recipes we regularly cook – whether entertaining friends or having simple family meals, indoors or al fresco, modest or grand. There's something here for every occasion, every season.

We like to bring out the inherent tastes of the ingredients, not mask them with exotic combinations of flavours. To make these recipes you will not have to waste your time buying a myriad different items, neither will you have to spend hours arranging them daintily on a plate. You won't be left wondering what all the competing flavours add up to, and you won't find odd mixtures of chocolate and blue cheese, or coconut ice cream and fried onions. There are no lists of peculiar store cupboard ingredients, and no need for complicated equipment.

While it's important for talented chefs to continue experimenting to keep culinary culture alive and well, we often feel like mice in test laboratories when faced with their groundbreaking concoctions. So most of our recipes here lean towards the traditional, tried and tested classics, the dishes you long for when you have been living on the culinary edge. Leave the complexity of fusion, the surgical methods and the mutant permutations of ingredients to those chefs who revel in pioneering cuisine. Certainly some stargazing chefs are producing extraordinary and interesting food with complex and challenging flavours. We don't decry this, but we feel that it's usually not the sort of food you want to eat very often and probably not at home.

Our type of food is not particularly fashionable nor is it unfashionable. We make full use of butter, cream, eggs, goose fat, olive oil, dripping, meat and game, and feel no guilt about indulging in these pleasures. Moderation and balance are the key here. It wouldn't be at all good for one, or indeed pleasurable, to eat roast beef with all the trimmings, every day, but every now and then it is an eagerly anticipated treat. Offset the days of rich intemperance with days of lighter fare.

Climate pays a part in what ingredients are on offer at particular times of the year. Hearty braises and root vegetables on chilly winter days, light dishes, salads and young vegetables during summer. Autumn, that 'season of mists and mellow fruitfulness' brings us game and orchard fruits. Take advantage of what each season has to offer and make use of it. This is a measure of economy too, when things are glutting, the price generally reflects the fact that the supply outweighs the demand. We make no apologies for consuming vast quantities of asparagus – English asparagus – during its short season.

Golden Raspberries

We long for the baby broad beans and peas of early summer, the golden raspberries of autumn. The thought of roast grouse, rib-sticking steak and kidney pudding, roast parsnips and braised endives make us almost look forward to winter. There's something wrong about eating strawberries in December – Paul Bocuse remarked that they taste of the grave. Hydroponically-grown tomatoes in February are fairly flavourless as is year-round asparagus, flown in from goodness knows where. The fact we can buy almost every ingredient all year round means that the food tastes of very little. It has generally spent too much time in gas-filled containers or chilled storage.

The ingredients used in these recipes can be found, with a little care, in many local greengrocer's, fishmonger's or butcher's shops, most good supermarkets, farmers' markets, or if you are lucky, your own vegetable plot. After some years of neglecting the flavour factor in food there seems to be a welcome recognition by some of the large supermarket operators that tasteless, aqua-grown vegetables, looking gleamingly perfect on their shelves, have had their day.

It's important to seek out suppliers of good raw ingredients. You will probably have to pay more for them because the supermarkets and farmers have in the past been convinced that price and quantity mattered more than quality. They concentrated on the mass-production of food at the lowest possible cost with maximum profit.

We fully realise as affluent middle-class authors it's easy to overlook the fact that for millions of hungry people the cost and quantity of food really does matter. For that reason we would certainly not criticise scientific experimentation, which can lead to increased crops, disease resistance, or add much needed vitamins to an otherwise deficient food source. Let's hope the scientists will not forget that flavour still matters.

Our kitchen in the country where we have done the preparation and cooking for all the recipes shown in this book is large or even very large. The kitchen proper is at one end and is equipped with a two-hob and four-oven Aga, and four electric hot plates. We don't have an overhead grill but we have the benefit of a waist-high wood-fired grill built into the chimneybreast. There is a fireplace at the other end of the room and a huge, solid oak table that seats ten easily.

We have a separate scullery where all the washing up takes place and which also stores the china and glass. One big asset is a north-facing larder with slate shelves, which stores most of the food – fresh, bottled, canned and packaged.

However, by far our greatest luxury is the enormous walled vegetable garden and orchard just by the back door. It's a real kitchen garden, growing every imaginable vegetable, herb and fruit, soft and hard, and tended by our indefatigable gardener, Jonathan Chidsey.

This wealth of fresh vegetables and fruit, coupled with eggs from hens, geese and ducks gives us a huge advantage. Remember, though, that even a small garden or allotment can produce a considerable flow of produce for the pot and help you to appreciate the different flavour you get from really fresh seasonal vegetables.

Our kitchen equipment is plain, simple and robust. We have very few gadgets apart from a Braun Multipractic. The array of pots and pans has been acquired over the years and among our favourites are a collection of heavy, copper pans and a couple of small silver saucepans. We have a number of wooden chopping boards of different sizes made from hardwood off-cuts from Benchmark's furniture factory, which occupies the old farm buildings next to the house.

Our china is usually white and our glassware clear. They are also rather plain as we think food looks better when it's not challenged by too much extraneous decoration; maybe a coloured band or the odd crest or sprig now and again on a plate adds a bit of charm or quirkiness.

We have a large collection of white, oval porcelain dishes – these are perfect for bringing food to the table as they hold the heat. We also have rather too many sharp carbon-steel knives and a few stainless steel ones, lots of wooden spoons and spatulas, sieves and colanders. An Aga kettle, scales and wire salad baskets more or less complete the collection. We miss the sensitivity of gas for cooking and particularly the lack of a grill, but we don't complain – the kitchen is certainly the hub of our home.

The intention of this book is to give guidance. While there are quantities listed, oven temperatures cited, and cooking times suggested, we would encourage you to be intuitive, to experiment, to taste what you are cooking and make adjustments to suit your palate. Don't be a slave to weights and measures, cooking is not an exact science, after all, how large is an onion? How hot is a wood-fired grill?

Preparing and cooking should not be seen as a chore, rather a productive activity, the results of which you can share with family and friends. Don't be inhibited by lack of skill, be prepared to make mistakes. While preparing and cooking the food for the photographs in this book, Vicki managed to forget things that were in the oven on a couple of occasions – charred chard gratin. The more you cook, the more confidence you will gain. Above all enjoy what you are doing and take pride in the meals you produce.

This book would not have been written without the inspiration of Elizabeth David, who brought sunshine, olive oil, the smell, taste and beauty of Mediterranean food to a grim and bruised post-war Britain. She showed us an alternative to tough over-cooked meat, grey watery vegetables, thick brown gravy and Spam fritters. She drew our attention to the invaluable advice given by the prolific and respected Escoffier: *faites simple*.

To start

Although intended as starters, most of the dishes in this chapter can be expanded to provide light main courses. Indeed, soups are generally so filling that, when accompanied by bread, butter and cheese, they make a substantial meal in themselves.

There are also starters for which no recipe is necessary, such as a plate of charcuterie. Delicious salamis, cured hams from France, Spain or Italy, terrines and pâtés with cornichons and bread are a wonderful and easy way to provide an appetising start to a meal. Smoked fish – cod's roe, eel, trout as well as the more ubiquitous salmon, are equally easy and delicious, accompanied by bread, capers, soured cream, horseradish or lemons.

The larder, too, can provide an array of starters – especially useful for feeding unexpected guests. Anchovies, canned or bottled, served with finely sliced onions, toasted bread and unsalted butter make an appetising beginning. Good Portuguese sardines, smoked cod's roe, stuffed olives, jars of marinated vegetables like artichokes and pimentos all make perfectly acceptable starters and are good store cupboard standbys.

It's worth keeping a few speciality breads in the freezer. When heated in the oven or toaster pita, brioche, focaccia and ciabatta not only smell delicious but are considerably more convenient than trying to bake from scratch, or dashing out to the baker or supermarket for fresh supplies.

Soupe à l'Oignon (gratinée)

This soup, a classic dish that was often eaten at Les Halles when it was a proper Parisian market, is just as delicious without the croûtons and Gruyère. When the weather is really cold, though, there's nothing as warming as a piping hot soup, golden-crusted and fragrantly steaming.

50g butter
4 large sweet onions, very finely sliced
2 garlic cloves, very finely sliced
1 teaspoon sugar
salt and pepper
1 litre light veal or vegetable stock
1 glass of dry white wine
a sprig of thyme and a few parsley stalks tied together

For the gratinée topping (optional):
4 slices of bread cut from a baguette, slightly dried in a coolish oven
100g grated Gruyère cheese

Melt the butter in a large saucepan then add the onions and garlic and sweat down very slowly until they are pale gold. This will take at least 30 minutes on a very low heat. The onions must not catch or burn. When they have gone a bit droopy, add the sugar and 1 teaspoon salt then continue to cook until they have shrunk a lot and are entirely wilted.

Add the stock, wine and herbs, then cook for a further 30 minutes. Taste and season as necessary.

If you want to make Soupe à l'Oignon Gratinée, pour the soup into small marmite soup bowls, add a slice of the dried bread to each bowl, top with a generous amount of grated Gruyère and place under a preheated hot grill until the cheese has melted and turned to molten gold. Be very careful – this soup takes ages to cool down; onions have a remarkable ability to retain heat for an immoderate length of time, and the cheese and bread have very efficient insulating properties.

Bisque

We always make this after we have eaten lobsters, prawns, crayfish or crabs, using the shells and left-over bits.

- 2 lobster or crab shells, or as many prawn or crayfish shells as will fit in the pot, together with the remaining leg, claw and body parts
- ½ wineglass of brandy or Armagnac
- 1 onion, roughly chopped
- 1 carrot, roughly chopped
- 1 stick of celery, chopped
- 1 tablespoon tomato purée
- 1 glass of white wine
- 1 to 2 dashes of anchovy essence
- bouquet garni – parsley, thyme, sage and bay leaf
- salt and pepper
- cayenne pepper, to serve
- Jersey cream – optional, to serve

Preheat the oven to 200°C (400°F), Gas Mark 6. Put the shells and other bits and pieces together in a roasting tin and place them in the oven for about 15 minutes until they are slightly charred.

Take the tin out of the oven, pour the brandy or Armagnac over the shells and ignite. When the flames have died down, tip the lot into a flameproof casserole with the onion, carrot, celery, tomato purée, wine, anchovy essence, bouquet garni and enough water to cover. Bring to the boil and simmer for 2 hours.

Remove the larger pieces of shell, and then blend the liquid with a strong blender. Strain through a conical sieve. Depending on how gravelly you like your bisque, add a spoonful or two of the sludgy shell left in the sieve. Adjust the seasoning and add a dash or two more of anchovy essence.

Serve very hot with a sprinkling of cayenne pepper. For a luxurious velvety touch add a spoonful or two of cream.

Leek and Potato Soup

Served either hot as Leek and Potato Soup or cold as Vichyssoise, these flavours are a brilliant combination, making soup that can be hot, hearty and robust or cool, smooth and sophisticated. The most important thing is to use only the white part of the leeks – the green, though lovely when raw, has a tendency to turn sludgy grey when cooked. Throw the green into the stockpot instead.

50g butter
600g leeks – just the white part – sliced
200g floury potatoes, peeled and sliced
500 ml chicken stock (see page 247), or vegetable stock (see page 246)
salt and pepper
a scrape of nutmeg
500 ml full fat milk
120ml double cream
double cream and chopped chives, to serve Vichyssoise

Melt the butter in a large, heavy-bottomed saucepan then add the leeks and turn them over in the butter. Let the leeks sweat over a low heat until they are softened and not at all brown. This will take about 12 to 15 minutes.

Add the potatoes to the leeks and turn them over in the pan for a few minutes. Pour in the stock, bring to a simmer and cook for about 20 minutes.

Season the soup with salt and pepper and a scrape of nutmeg. If you want a robust soup just mash the solids with a potato masher, stopping when you achieve the texture you want. Add the milk and cream and bring to simmering point.

To make Vichyssoise, purée the soup, either in a blender or with one of those hand-held devices specially made for the job. We like to then push the soup through the finest sieve of a mouli-legumes, or a conical strainer for a really smooth and velvety finish. Chill until needed.

Remember to adjust the seasoning before you serve the Vichyssoise – cold soups sometimes need a bit of perking up. Serve in chilled soup plates. All it needs is a swirl of cream and some chopped chives.

Borscht

Beetroot never fails to amaze – that the depth and intensity of its colour is achieved in the garden is one of nature's miracles. Borscht, one of Russia's better-known culinary exports, is the classic beetroot soup. The earthy flavour is complemented by a good rich beef stock. Served hot in the winter, it is equally good chilled as a summer soup. Whatever, the colour is ravishing and demands the purest white soup plates.

50g butter
250g beetroot, peeled and roughly chopped
1 onion, chopped
1 carrot, chopped
3 garlic cloves, chopped
1 tablespoon sugar
1½ litres beef stock (see page 246)
salt and pepper
juice of ½ lemon
soured cream, to serve
a handful of chopped chives, to garnish

Melt the butter in a large pan, over a gentle heat and slowly sweat the beetroot, onion, carrot and garlic, turning the vegetables (which will become a lurid pink) over in the butter.

Add the sugar and stock to the pan, season with a few grinds of pepper, bring the soup to a simmer and cook for about 40 minutes until the vegetables are tender.

Using a blender, whizz the soup until it is entirely smooth, then add the lemon juice and salt to taste. A swirl of soured cream and a scattering of chopped chives is the traditional garnish – delicious, and adding another dimension to the fabulous beetroot colour.

Consommé

Intense, clear and elegant, consommé is comforting and nourishing without being at all heavy. You can adapt the basic recipe to make variations on the theme of clear soup – beetroot makes a wonderful jewel-like soup, tomato captures the essential flavour of ripe tomatoes, watercress delivers a punchy green. Serve this soup hot or cold, in which case it sets to a limpid jelly.

2 unpeeled onions, halved
1 chicken, free-range, weighing about 1.5kg
1 calf's foot, chopped (by your butcher)
2 carrots, roughly chopped
2 celery sticks, roughly chopped
2 leeks, sliced
300ml white wine
10 black peppercorns
½ tablespoon salt
a bunch of parsley stalks
a bay leaf and a sprig of thyme
2 egg whites
salt

Preheat the oven to 220°C (425°F), Gas Mark 7.

Put the onion halfs in the oven for 15 minutes until slightly toasted on the cut surface and the skins are dark brown. This gives the stock a good golden colour.

Put the onion and all the remaining ingredients, except the egg whites and salt, into a large flameproof casserole and bring to a simmer. Leave to cook gently for 2–2½ hours.

Remove the chicken from the broth and reserve it for another meal. Strain the broth into a clean pan and skim the fat from the surface.

Allow the broth to cool a little then whisk in the egg whites over a gentle heat while a nice foamy crust forms on the surface. Stop whisking and allow the broth to blip away at a simmer for 30 minutes.

Remove from the heat, and, with a slotted spoon or skimmer, lift the crust from the surface. Strain the now clear broth through two layers of muslin to catch any remaining impurities.

Taste and add salt if necessary. Refrigerate until you want to use it.

Tomato Consommé

Towards the end of the summer when tomatoes are at their best, this is one of the most delicious soups you can make. It can be served hot or chilled.

2kg ripe tomatoes, coarsely chopped
1 small onion, finely chopped
2 garlic cloves, finely chopped
salt and pepper

Put the tomatoes, together with the onion and garlic, a splash of water, a pinch of salt and a couple of grinds of black pepper, in a heavy-bottomed pan. Place over a low heat and let the tomatoes collapse – they should not boil, and try to resist stirring them. Depending on the ripeness of the tomatoes, this could take 30–45 minutes.

When the tomatoes have become liquid, carefully tip them into a large colander lined with muslin and suspended over a clean pan, and leave for the liquid to drip through. If you have managed to resist bashing the tomatoes up by stirring or squishing the pulp through the colander, the resulting liquid should be clear. Taste it and if you think it is a bit thin, put it back on the heat and reduce until the strength of flavour you want is reached.

Gazpacho

Another summer soup, essentially served very, very cold. It couldn't be simpler – no stock, all you need is a good liquidizer and lots of ice.

1 cucumber, peeled and coarsely chopped, plus extra to garnish
2 red peppers, halved, cored, deseeded and coarsely chopped
2 garlic cloves, chopped
4 spring onions, coarsely chopped
6 very ripe tomatoes, skinned and deseeded
100g fresh breadcrumbs
a small splash of red wine vinegar
a large splash of olive oil
salt and pepper
about 500ml crushed ice

Put the cucumber in the bowl of a food processor with the red peppers, garlic and spring onions and whizz until finely chopped. Add the tomatoes, breadcrumbs and vinegar and whizz again, adding the olive oil until the soup is rather thicker than you would want it. Add salt and pepper to taste, remembering that the finished soup will be somewhat diluted with ice. Put the soup in the fridge to chill.

Before you serve the soup, preferably in a large glass or white china bowl, stir in the ice and garnish with chopped cucumber.

Chowder

Almost a fish stew, chowder can be as hearty and robust as you want it. It has great flexibility in that it can be made from many combinations of fish, shellfish or crustacea. There are two main chowder variations: New England-style, which is milk based and therefore white, and New York-style which, being tomato based, is red. We've given here a New England-style smoked fish chowder, but the ingredients can be varied to suit the season or occasion – we particularly like shellfish such as clams and crabmeat, or, for a special occasion, lobster.

50g butter
100g streaky bacon, diced
1 onion, chopped
1 stick of celery, chopped
2 leeks, white part only, chopped
1 large potato, peeled and diced
400g smoked white fish – haddock or cod
500ml milk – full fat
1 bay leaf
about 500ml of fish stock or water
2 tablespoons parsley, finely chopped
salt and white pepper

Melt the butter in a large casserole and sauté the bacon. Add the onion, celery, leeks and potato to the casserole and sweat them slowly until the vegetables have softened.

Meanwhile, put the fish into a shallow pan with the milk, bay leaf and enough of the stock or water to cover, and simmer slowly for about 10 minutes. Remove the fish from the pan and allow to cool. Strain the cooking liquid over the bacon and vegetables and bring to a simmer.

Discard the skin, and any bones from the fish, then flake the flesh, adding it, with the parsley, to the casserole. Taste, add salt if needed, and season with white pepper.

Serve the soup in very hot plates, with crusty bread, or croûtons fried in clarified butter. Traditionally, crumbled water biscuits were added to thicken the broth.

For a New York-style chowder, substitute the same amount of skinned, deseeded and chopped plum tomatoes for the milk.

Pea and Ham Soup

This is best made towards the end of the season, with fresh peas that are just becoming slightly floury. In the winter months when fresh peas are not available, soaked split peas or frozen peas work well.

50g butter
1 onion, chopped
1kg shelled peas
1 litre ham or gammon stock, or chicken stock (see page 247)
100g cooked ham or gammon, finely diced
salt and pepper
Jersey cream, to serve

Melt the butter in a saucepan and sweat the onion until soft. Add the peas (or soaked split peas, or frozen peas) and turn them over in the butter for a minute.

Pour the stock into the pan and bring to a boil, then simmer for about 20 minutes until tender (split peas will need about 40 minutes).

Purée the soup in a blender, add the ham or gammon, then adjust the seasoning. Serve really hot, with a swirl of cream on top.

Scotch Broth

Not a soup to be made in a hurry. It is essential to let the lamb cool in the stock, thus enabling you to lift a dinner-plate of solidified fat off it. Traditionally made with mutton, it is perfectly acceptable to use lamb – forequarter cuts like neck are best for a long cooking.

750g best end of neck of lamb
a sprig of thyme
a bay leaf
100g dried split or whole peas
200g carrots, diced
200g leeks, sliced
200g potatoes, diced
2 onions, chopped
1 celery stalk, diced
1 small turnip or swede, diced
50g pearl barley
½ cabbage, shredded finely
salt and white pepper
a handful of finely chopped parsley

Put the lamb in a large pan with enough water to easily cover. Bring to the boil and skim off the scum that forms. Lower the heat to a simmer, add the thyme and bay leaf, and allow to cook slowly for about 1 to 1½ hours until the meat is tender.

When the lamb is cooked, leave the pan in a cool place overnight. Put the peas to soak in plenty of cold water.

The following day you will find that you will be able to lift off the fat from the lamb very easily. Discard the bones from the lamb and break the meat up into sensible soup-sized pieces.

At least 1 hour before you want to serve the soup, add the vegetables (except the cabbage), barley and drained soaked peas to the pan and cook gently for 1 hour, adding the cabbage towards the end of this time.

Season with salt and white pepper, and add chopped parsley just before serving.

A meal in itself, all Scotch broth needs is the accompaniment of good bread and butter, and perhaps a bit of English cheese – something like Swaledale or a farmhouse single Gloucester.

Foie Gras

The rich, buttery liver from geese or ducks, force-fed on maize, is one of the great culinary luxuries. The purposeful fattening of the birds was done as early as Roman times, when wheat and barley were supplemented with figs. Whether to go for goose or duck liver is entirely dependent on personal taste – goose liver being finer and having a more delicate flavour. When buying duck foie gras cru *(raw) look for a putty-coloured, smooth and rounded liver, weighing about 300–400g. Michel Guérard makes the most voluptuous pot au feu imaginable using a whole foie gras gently poached in broth, served with tiny vegetables – quite outstanding and well worth a trip to Eugénie-les-Bains.*

1 duck liver
½ teaspoon salt
½ teaspoon black pepper
50ml Sauternes
50ml Armagnac

Allow the liver to come to room temperature to make it easier to handle. Very gently and carefully remove the veins, tubes and membrane from the liver. A very thin-bladed craft knife or a scalpel is useful for this rather surgical procedure. Sprinkle the liver with salt and pepper. At this stage you could add some slivers of truffle if you have some, tucking them into the natural folds of the liver.

Choose a ceramic terrine in which the liver will fit quite snugly and gently ease it in. Cover with the Sauternes and Armagnac, then with a lid or aluminium foil and refrigerate overnight.

The next day take the dish from the fridge and again allow it to come to room temperature. Preheat the oven to 110°C (225°F), Gas Mark ¼.

Half-fill a roasting tin with hot water and stand the terrine in it. Place it in the oven for 20 minutes.

Remove the terrine from the roasting tin then chill. There should be a layer of delicious yellow fat on the surface which helps to keep the foie gras fresh.

Serve very cold with toast – brioche is a rather fabulous alternative, being light and slightly sweet.

Chicken Liver Terrine

This recipe gives a rather coarse terrine, nice with crusty baguette and cornichons. It keeps well in the fridge, in fact it seems to mature and get better a couple of days after cooking. In the winter you can add pieces of game birds – pheasant or partridge; just cook the terrine for a bit longer.

20g butter
1 onion, finely chopped
2 garlic cloves, crushed
300g chicken livers, finely chopped
50g pork fat, cut into little cubes
50g soft white breadcrumbs
a scrape of nutmeg
a couple of juniper berries, crushed
a splash of Cognac
1 egg, beaten
salt and pepper
150g pork fat, cut into thin slices
1 to 2 bay leaves – optional

Heat the butter in a pan and sauté the onion until soft.

Transfer the onion to a large bowl, add all the remaining ingredients – except the sliced back fat and bay leaves – and mix thoroughly. You can leave this mixture for about 24 hours in the fridge.

Preheat the oven to 170°C (325°F), Gas Mark 3.

Line a 800-ml to 1-litre terrine with the slices of pork fat, keeping a couple of slices to make a cover.

Put the mixture into the lined terrine, smooth the top and lay the remaining strips of fat on top. You can put a bay leaf or two on top if you like. Cover with a lid or a couple of sheets of foil and place in a roasting tin half-filled with water in the oven for 1 hour. Remove from the oven, and place some weights on top of the terrine. Allow to cool then refrigerate.

Rabbit Terrine

Serves about 16

a 1.5kg to 2kg rabbit with its liver

For the marinade:

50ml olive oil
a squeeze of lemon juice
a sprig of thyme
a sprig of rosemary
a sprig of sage
3 or 4 bay leaves
pepper

For the terrine:

2 garlic cloves, crushed
50g fresh breadcrumbs
50g pistachio nuts, shelled and chopped
300g pork back fat, finely cubed
200g streaky bacon, finely cubed
200g chicken breast, minced
the rabbit's liver, minced
2 large eggs, beaten
50ml Cognac or Armagnac
a pinch each of allspice, white pepper and cloves
a scrape of nutmeg
1 teaspoon salt
300g pork back fat, cut into thin slices
2 bay leaves

Mix the marinade ingredients together. Remove the meat from the rabbit, keeping the back fillets and the white leg meat in large pieces. Put them in a bowl, pour over the marinade, cover and leave in a cool place overnight. Then remove the meat from the bowl, reserving the marinade.

Preheat the oven to 180°C (350°F), Gas Mark 4.

Take the rest of the meat from the carcass, chop it finely and add it to the garlic, breadcrumbs, pistachios, cubed fat, bacon, the minced chicken breast and rabbit's liver. Mix well then add the eggs, Cognac or Armagnac, the spices, marinade and salt.

Line a terrine, about 2 litre capacity, with the slices of pork back fat, reserving some to cover the terrine. Start filling the terrine with the minced mixture, then lay in some of the pieces of white meat. Cover with the remaining mixture and knock the terrine on a hard surface to level the contents. Cover with the reserved slices of back fat and press the bay leaves on top. Cover with a lid or a piece of aluminium foil.

Place the terrine in a roasting tin half-filled with hot water and cook in the oven for 1½ to 2 hours, until the juices on the surface are clear. Then remove from the oven and put the terrine on a platter.

Have ready a piece of heavy card, cut to the size of the top of the terrine and wrapped in several layers of foil, and place on top of the cooked terrine. Place some weights on top – a couple of cans of tomatoes – and allow to cool completely. Quite a lot of juice will escape – do not be alarmed.

Take off the weights, remove the foil-wrapped card and cover the terrine with the lid. Refrigerate until needed.

Jambon Persillée

This dish of shreds of pink ham suspended in a green-flecked jelly is one of the prettiest and tastiest of summer terrines. It makes a nice light lunch dish served with a crisp salad of Little Gem lettuce.

1 ham hock, weighing about 1kg
1 pig's trotter – have the butcher split it
1 onion, sliced
1 carrot, sliced
1 stick of celery, sliced
a bunch of parsley stalks
10 white peppercorns
300ml white wine
a splash of white wine vinegar
a large handful of parsley, finely chopped

Put the ham hock, trotter, onion, carrot, celery, parsley stalks and white peppercorns in a large pan with the wine, vinegar and enough water to cover. Bring to a simmer and cook gently for 1½ hours until the ham is falling off the bone.

Remove all the meat from the hock and break it up with two forks, putting it into a ceramic basin. Stir in the parsley.

Strain the cooking liquid through two layers of muslin and allow it to cool.

Remove the fat from the surface of the cooled stock, which should by now be turning to light jelly; pour this on the ham and mix gently but well. Turn it into a ceramic or enamelled terrine and refrigerate.

Serve the terrine with crusty bread, cornichons or a crisp green salad.

Chicken and Ham Pie

Very simple and extremely satisfying, this pie is ideal as a starter, or for picnics or al fresco lunches. You can use any combination of pork and game for the filling.

250g pork belly fat, chopped
200g chicken thigh meat, chopped
a handful of finely chopped parsley, tarragon and chervil
salt and pepper
50ml strong chicken stock (see page 247)
250g gammon, cut into strips
250g chicken breast, cut into strips
1 egg yolk beaten with 1 tablespoon milk

For the pastry:
160g lard
450g plain flour
½ teaspoon salt

To finish:
300ml well-flavoured, clear, jellied chicken stock (see page 247)

Mix the pork belly, chicken thigh meat, herbs, salt, pepper and chicken stock. To make the pastry, put the lard and 250ml water into a saucepan and heat gently. When the lard has melted, bring to the boil and immediately tip in the flour and salt. Mix well with a wooden spoon to bring the pastry together. Cover with a tea towel until cool enough to handle.

Preheat the oven to 200°C (400°F), Gas Mark 6.

Leaving a quarter of the pastry covered and warm, roll out the larger piece and put it into a hinged pie mould or a 2 litre springform cake tin. Line the tin – the pastry will be malleable enough to press it up the sides with your fingers. The thicker the pastry, the stronger the pie shell will be.

Put layers of the chopped meat and the gammon and breast strips into the pie, pressing down as you go. Roll out the remaining quarter of the pastry to make a lid for the pie.

Wet the edges of the pie and cover with the lid, pressing the edges to seal. Cut a vent hole in the centre and trim the edges of the pie; flute them if you like, with fingers or the tines of a fork.

Brush the pie with the egg wash and bake for 30 minutes. Lower the heat to 160°C (325°F), Gas Mark 2, and cook the pie for a further 1½ hours. If the top looks too brown, cover it with some kitchen foil.

Take the pie out of the oven and very carefully remove the sides of the tin. Brush the sides of the pie with egg wash and put it back in the oven for 10 to 15 minutes to brown the sides. Remove from the oven and allow to cool.

To finish, warm the jellied stock so that it is just liquid and, using a small funnel, carefully pour it into the pie through the hole in the lid. This fills the gaps between the filling and the pastry that occur due to the shrinkage of the meat during cooking. Refrigerate for 24 hours before eating.

clockwise from top left: When making the pastry, keep stirring the flour and melted lard mixture until it forms a dough. Once cooled, knead the mixture, then roll it out. Press the pastry into the pie mould. **page 34 and 35:** To make the pie lid, roll out the remaining dough, then fold it in half and cut a small triangle from the folded edge. When opened out, this will leave a diamond-shaped hole through which excess steam can escape. Press the pastry lid to the base then brush with egg wash.

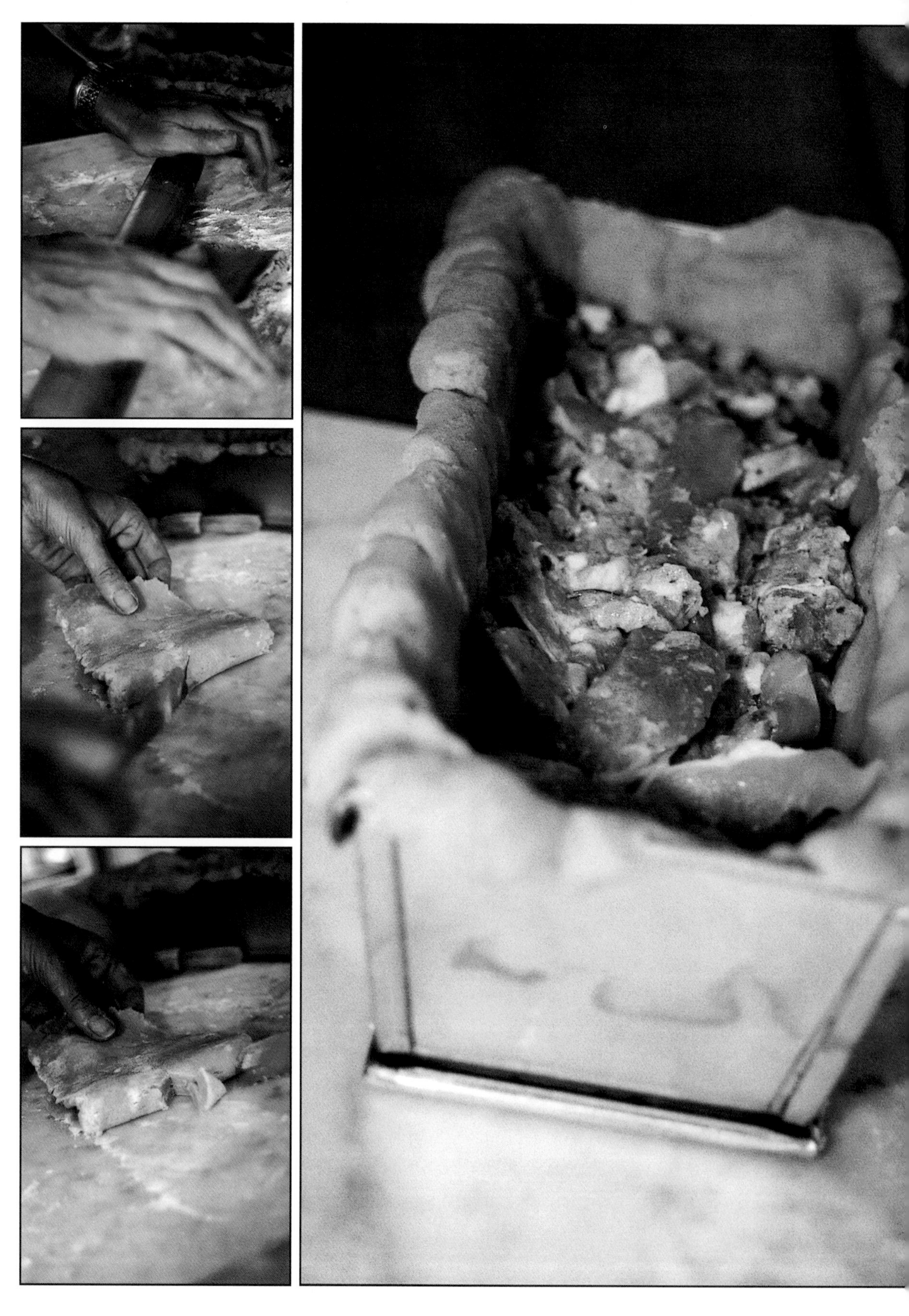

Tomato Salad

We're very keen on tomato salad – it has a surprising number of variations: with a plain vinaigrette or a mustard dressing, with finely chopped shallots or garlic, anchovies or olives, with torn-up basil leaves, or just excellent olive oil. The important thing is to get really good flavoursome tomatoes; supermarkets sell tomatoes actually labelled 'grown for flavour' – do they grow others for doing the ironing, helping with homework or their ability to hang wallpaper?

4 large, 6 medium or 8 small tomatoes
a pinch each of sugar and salt
a few grinds of pepper
good olive oil
a splash of red wine vinegar

With a sharp knife cut out the core of each tomato then plunge the tomatoes into boiling water for about 30 seconds. Refresh the tomatoes in cold water and peel them. This is really important – in fact we get really cross when we get tomatoes with the skins on in a restaurant. The exception would be really sweet small tomatoes like Gardener's Delight.

Slice the tomatoes thickly and place them on a shallow dish. Sprinkle with the sugar, salt and pepper and leave for about 15 minutes. Simply dress with some good olive oil and a splash of red wine vinegar.

Celeriac Rémoulade

A classic of the Routier restaurants of France, celeriac rémoulade is a really fine starter, especially when accompanying some Jambon de Montagne or Bayonne.

1 celeriac root, weighing about 800g
juice of 1 lemon
salt
1 egg yolk
2 tablespoons Dijon mustard
150ml olive oil
splash of red wine vinegar
a handful of chopped parsley

Fill a bowl with water and add the lemon juice. Peel and grate or shred the celeriac, immediately putting it into the acidulated water. This will stop it turning brown.

Bring a pan of salted water to the boil and plunge in the celeriac. Return to the boil then drain in a colander, shaking it to remove as much water as possible.

Meanwhile, mix the egg yolk, mustard and a pinch of salt together in a nice roomy bowl, using a little balloon whisk or a wooden spoon.

Start adding the oil, a dribble to start with, beating well, until the oil is absorbed. As the mixture becomes more emulsified, you can start adding the oil in a more steady stream until it becomes thick and golden. Add a splash of vinegar to taste, and to slacken the sauce.

When the celeriac is cold and dry, fold it, with the parsley, into the mayonnaise.

Little Gem Lettuces with Salad Cream

A really simple and delicious salad. Salad cream is a dressing that has fallen into disrepute, possibly because of commercial varieties that taste rather harsh and nasty. When made with good ingredients, it is a really lovely light and summery way to dress a salad, and a pleasing alternative to vinaigrette.

4 Little Gem lettuces
1 teaspoon sugar
1 teaspoon salt
a pinch of white pepper
1 teaspoon mustard
1 tablespoon white wine vinegar
4 tablespoons thin cream
a few drops of walnut oil

Take any tough leaves off then cut the lettuces into quarters, laying them on a shallow serving dish.

Mix the sugar, salt, pepper, mustard and vinegar together. Gradually add the cream, stirring vigorously to prevent the mixture splitting. Add a few drops of walnut oil and drizzle over the lettuces.

Salad Niçoise

Possibly the most disputed recipe of modern times. Do you add anchovies, peppers, lettuce, tuna, tomatoes, artichokes… or not? The alleged definitive recipe, by Jean Medecin, the notorious mayor of Nice, uses only cooked vegetables, while Larousse Gastronomique *suggests the addition of peppers, celery and onions. Whatever, it is a delicious combination, but we tend to go for a 'less is more' philosophy. And always use good, oil-packed, canned tuna from Spain or Portugal. The fondness of fashionable restaurants for using grilled fresh tuna is missing the point of both tuna and Salade Niçoise. Here's our version.*

250g fine French beans, topped and tailed
250g small new potatoes
4 ripe tomatoes, skinned and quartered
250g canned tuna, drained and flaked
4 eggs, hard-boiled and halved
6 anchovy fillets
250g olives – those nice little olives from Nice are ideal
lettuce hearts, to serve

For the vinaigrette:
1 tablespoon red wine vinegar
1 teaspoon Dijon mustard
1 garlic clove, minced
4 tablespoons olive oil

Cook the beans in salted water until tender then refresh in iced water. Cook the potatoes in a similar way then, when cool enough to handle, slice them and leave to cool completely.

Arrange the beans, potatoes and tomatoes on a large platter, then add the tuna together with the eggs, anchovy fillets and olives. To make the vinaigrette, whisk the ingredients together, then drizzle over the salad.

Serve some lettuce hearts separately.

Charcuterie

Charcuterie, literally cooked meat – *chair cuit* – goes back a long way in the history of food, the charcutiers were organised into a guild in the fifteenth century. We now think of charcuterie as being salamis, saucisses and other cured meats. They are available in a wide variety from all over Europe – France, Italy and Germany. Increasingly Spanish, Polish, Austrian and British specialities are available in delicatessens and supermarkets.

A selection of charcuterie makes an excellent and easy starter. Choose saucissons secs from France – rosette and jesus de Lyon, saucisson de montagne, d'Arles; salamis from Italy – Napoli and Milan, or finely sliced mortadella; wursts from Germany and spicy chorizo from Spain. Serve with crusty bread, cornichons, caper berries, olives or mustard fruits. Raw ham makes an elegant light meal, Proscuitto di Parma is probably the best known raw ham and simply delicious served with figs, melon or shavings of Parmesan cheese.

Spain produces many hams, jamon iberico, known also as *pata negra*, is from native Spanish pigs reared in the oak forests of southern Spain and is known for its fine flavour, attributed to the acorns the pigs habitually eat. France's jambon de Bayonne and jambon de Montagne are good rustic hams, great with cornichons, unsalted butter and pain paysan. German hams are generally heavily smoked, though Westphalian ham is delicate, having been smoked over juniper wood. Try a selection of sausage and hams, allowing about 200g per person as a starter, or 300g for a light lunch dish.

Endive and Roquefort Salad

Couldn't be easier, or more delicious. There's something about the combination of the slightly bitter, cool endives, the rich creamy sharpness of Roquefort and the bite of walnuts that is very satisfying. We like it with a light mustard dressing, but a sprinkling of olive oil and a squeeze of lemon is also very good.

4 Belgian endives
150 g Roquefort
120g walnuts

For the dressing:
2 tsps mustard
4 tbsp olive oil
2 tbsp lemon juice
salt and pepper

Remove the leaves from each endive and pile them on a platter. Crumble the Roquefort and coarsely chop the walnuts. Scatter the cheese and nuts over the endive leaves.

Mix the dressing ingredients together and, just before serving, drizzle over the salad. Roquefort is quite salty, so go easy with the salt in the dressing.

Artichokes with Broad Beans

Needing no cooking at all, this depends on being able to get very, very young broad beans and tiny artichokes. Simply pod the beans and finely slice the artichokes then serve them with some olive oil, salt and lemon juice or some really good vinegar.

Cheese Soufflé

Not rocket science: a cheese soufflé is remarkably easy to make. The important thing to remember is that it won't wait around after it has finished cooking, so time your putting it into the oven so that everyone will be seated, forks ready, for when you bring it, golden, fluffy, creamy and delicious, to the table.

50g Parmesan cheese, grated
40g butter
40g flour
200ml milk, heated to just below boiling point
5 eggs, separated
a pinch of salt
75g Gruyère cheese, grated
a scrape of nutmeg
a pinch of cayenne pepper
a pinch of white pepper

Butter a 1½-litre soufflé dish and sprinkle in a teaspoonful or two of the grated Parmesan, shaking the dish so that the cheese is distributed over the bottom and around the sides.

Melt the butter in a large saucepan then stir in the flour and cook, stirring, over a gentle heat. Slowly pour in the milk and bring to the boil, stirring until the sauce has thickened. Take the pan off the heat.

In a large bowl, whisk the egg whites with a pinch of salt until they are thick, white and glossy.

Beat the egg yolks into the milky sauce and fold in the rest of the Parmesan, the Gruyère, nutmeg, cayenne and white pepper. Take a large tablespoon of egg white and quickly fold it into the sauce to slacken it. Then very carefully and lightly, using a spatula or a large metal spoon, fold the remaining egg whites into the mixture.

Turn the foamy mass into the buttered soufflé dish. At this stage you can cover the dish with a large bowl, upturned over it. Leave it in a warm place, out of a draught, for up to 1 hour.

Preheat the oven at 200°C (400°F), Gas Mark 6.

Thirty minutes before you are going to eat, put the soufflé into the oven. Do not open the door during the cooking time. It will be deep golden on top, while nicely risen and creamy within.

Oeufs Durs Mayonnaise

These eggs make a versatile starter – with mayonnaise (below), anchovies, sliced tomatoes, tapenade, lettuce, radishes, some cold poached fish, aïoli (see page 80) or asparagus. It is essential to use really good eggs – some shops sell Italian eggs that have the deepest yellow yolks and a really good flavour, otherwise go for free-range organic or specialist breeds. It's not necessary to have recently-laid eggs – if they are too fresh they will be really difficult to shell.

6 or 8 eggs

Put the eggs into a pan of cold water and bring to a simmer. Set your timer for 5 minutes if you like the yolks a bit creamy, or 7 minutes if you want them hard, and boil the eggs until the timer pings, buzzes or whatever. Take the pan off the heat and run cold water into it for a couple of minutes. Shell the eggs and leave to cool.

To serve, cut each egg in half and put, cut side up, on a dish.

Mayonnaise

The magical transformation of egg yolks and oil into a wonderful ointment is an amazing feat of science. We use olive oil, but any of the good light oils – grapeseed, safflower or light olive oil – make good mayonnaise. It is useful to have all the ingredients at room temperature – far less likely to split or curdle. If mayonnaise does curdle all is not lost; simply start afresh with a new egg yolk and some mustard, adding a small amount of oil, drop by drop, and when the mixture has started to thicken and stabilise, add the curdled mixture, a bit at a time, stirring vigorously. This should remedy the situation and make an even richer mayonnaise.

1 large egg yolk
1 teaspoon Dijon mustard
salt
about 200 to 250ml oil
a squeeze of lemon juice or a splash of white wine vinegar

Mix the egg yolk, mustard and salt together in a big bowl using a small balloon whisk, or a wooden spoon.

Start adding the oil, a dribble to start with, beating well, until the oil is absorbed. As the mixture becomes more emulsified, you can add the oil in a more steady stream. It will become thick and golden.

Slacken the sauce with a squeeze of lemon or a splash of vinegar to taste.

The mayonnaise will keep for a couple of days, covered, in a cool place, but we never have any left.

Oeufs en Gelée

We make this when we have some good chicken stock, some left-over egg whites, and some tarragon and really fresh eggs. It's a bit fiddly and time-consuming, but the finished dish is so ravishing it's worth the effort.

500ml well-flavoured, jellied chicken stock (see page 247)
1 to 2 egg whites
a small bunch of tarragon leaves, briefly blanched
8 very fresh eggs
lettuce leaves, to serve

Put the stock in a saucepan with the egg white(s). Over a gentle heat and using a small whisk, amalgamate the stock and the egg white(s) and allow to come to a simmer, then stop stirring. Let the stock blip away for about 15 minutes – a nice foamy crust will form on top and the liquid underneath should be crystal clear.

Remove the crust with a skimmer or slotted spoon, and ladle the stock into a bowl, through a muslin-lined sieve if there are still particles of egg white in the stock.

Pour a layer of stock into a dish large enough to accommodate all the eggs, lay some tarragon leaves on top and place the dish and the bowl of stock in the fridge.

Meanwhile, put a large shallow pan of water on to boil. When it is boiling, remove the pan from the heat and carefully break the eggs into the water. You may need to do this in batches, depending on how large your pan is. Cover the pan and allow it to sit for about 3 minutes.

Check to see if the eggs are firm enough to handle. The whites should be firm and the yolks soft. Leave the eggs for a little longer if you prefer them more well done. Using a slotted spoon, take the eggs, one at a time, from the water, allowing them to drain on a tea towel, and then place them on a plate. When all the eggs have been poached and drained, put the plate into the fridge.

When the jelly has set in the base of the dish and the eggs are cold, place the eggs on the jelly and put the dish back in the fridge to firm up.

When the remaining stock in the bowl has become syrupy, spoon it gently over the eggs, cover the dish with clingfilm and return it to the fridge.

Serve the eggs on chilled plates with some lettuce leaves.

If you serve the eggs for a lunch or dinner party, it's rather nice to put a sprig of tarragon, an egg and the stock into individual cocotte dishes or dariole moulds and, when set, turn them out onto the serving plates.

Since we use eggs from our own hens, we write on them with pencil to indicate the date they were laid. Poached eggs are best made using really fresh eggs, ideally less than a week old. To poach an egg, bring a large shallow pan of water to the boil. Remove the pan from the heat and carefully break the egg into the water. Put the lid on the pan and allow it to sit for about 3 minutes. Remove the poached egg from the water using a slotted spoon.

The jellied stock that is used to make Oeufs en Gelée is very simple to make – see the recipe on page 247.
Opposite, clockwise from top left: Put the stock in a saucepan with the egg whites. Over a gentle heat and using a small whisk, amalgamate the stock and the egg whites. Bring to a simmer, then stop stirring. Let the stock blip away for about 15 minutes – a foamy crust will form on top and the liquid beneath should be crystal clear.
Above, anti-clockwise from top left: Remove the crust with a slotted spoon, and ladle the stock into a bowl, through a muslin-lined sieve if there are still particles of egg white in it. As it cools the stock will become a jelly.

Omelette aux Fines Herbes

It is only really worth making an omelette if you are generous with the eggs. Two large or three small eggs per person is the minimum. Free-range organic eggs have a better taste; some commercially-produced eggs taste of fish – yeuck.

Serves 1

2 large or 3 medium eggs
a knob of butter
salt and pepper
1 teaspoon each of finely chopped parsley, tarragon, chervil and chives

In a bowl, lightly beat the eggs with 1 tablespoon cold water.

Melt the butter in an omelette pan until it is foaming. Add the seasoning and herbs to the eggs, then tip them into the pan. Fork the mixture gently until it starts to set, moving the cooked eggs into the centre so the uncooked egg can run to the edges.

When the omelette is nearly set, but still a bit runny in the centre, fold it in half, then slide the whole omelette onto a hot plate and eat immediately.

POUPON
PRODUIT DE FRANCE
PREPARED
DIJON

Leeks Vinaigrette

Leeks, when they are young and slender, make a nice light starter or cold vegetable accompaniment. If you can't get very thin leeks you can use larger, split lengthways.

8 slender leeks
2 eggs, hard-boiled, peeled and coarsely chopped

For the vinaigrette:
2 tablespoons red wine vinegar
120 ml olive oil
2 tablespoons Dijon mustard
salt and pepper

Put the leeks into a large shallow pan of lightly salted, boiling water and cook for about 7 to 10 minutes until tender.

Meanwhile, make the vinaigrette. Mix together the red wine vinegar, the olive oil and the Dijon mustard. Season the dressing with salt and pepper.

Remove the cooked leeks from the water and allow them to drain thoroughly. Arrange the leeks on a shallow dish and drizzle them with lots of vinaigrette. Strew the chopped eggs over the leeks and pour the rest of the vinaigrette over the finished dish.

Potted Shrimps

If you can get live shrimps, freshly boiled they make the most delicious potted shrimps. Cooked Morecambe Bay shrimps are also very good and easy to get from decent fishmongers. Indeed ready-potted shrimps can be very good as well.

250g clarified butter
a pinch of freshly ground mace
500g cooked shrimps, peeled
salt
a pinch of cayenne pepper

Melt half the clarified butter in a saucepan, add the ground mace and allow to sizzle for a moment.

Throw the shrimps into the pan and turn in the butter until they are well covered. Taste and add salt if it is needed then pack into ramekins. Sprinkle with the cayenne pepper.

Melt the remaining butter and pour over the shrimps. When the butter has cooled, place the ramekins in the fridge.

Serve the potted shrimps with hot toast.

Anchovies with Onions

Another no-fuss starter – simply finely slice a sweet Spanish onion and serve with really good, plump and pink, salted anchovies and some fine, unsalted butter and crusty bread.

Smoked Fish

A minimum-fuss meal can be made of an assortment of smoked fish – cod's roe, trout, eel and, of course, salmon, served with grated horseradish, soured cream, lemons and brown bread and butter. We once entertained eight Japanese businessmen for a working lunch, serving a large platter of smoked fish with a variety of breads and pickles to accompany it; they delightedly tucked into the fish, but appeared to be looking for something other than the pickles we had put out. Not knowing quite what they wanted we looked in the larder for something else – Marmite, mustard, honey, marmalade – yes, that was it – they wanted marmalade with their smoked fish.

Peppers Piedmontese

A lovely summer lunch dish, this is best served at room temperature with lots of crusty baguette to mop up the juices.

4 large ripe tomatoes
4 red peppers, halved, cored and deseeded
4 garlic cloves, very finely sliced
8 anchovy fillets
a good splash of olive oil
salt and pepper

Preheat the oven to 220°C (425°F), Gas Mark 7.

Using a sharp knife, remove the core from each tomato. Place the first tomato in a small bowl and pour in enough boiling water to cover it. Leave for 10 seconds, then pour away the hot water and fill the bowl with cold water. Remove the cooled tomato from the bowl and peel away the skin. It should slide off easily. Cut the tomato in half and repeat the process with the remaining three tomatoes.

Place the pepper halves in a baking dish, cut side up, and put an eighth of the garlic in each, followed by an anchovy fillet. Top with a tomato half, cut side down. Drizzle olive oil over the peppers and sprinkle on the salt and pepper. Place in the oven and, after about 15 minutes, just when the peppers start to char, turn the oven down to about 180°C (350°F), Gas Mark 4. Allow the peppers to cook for another 45 minutes to 1 hour until they are soft and starting to collapse. Leave the peppers to cool to room temperature.

Have these with a bowl of Niçoise olives and a rosé wine from Bandol and you could almost be in the south of France.

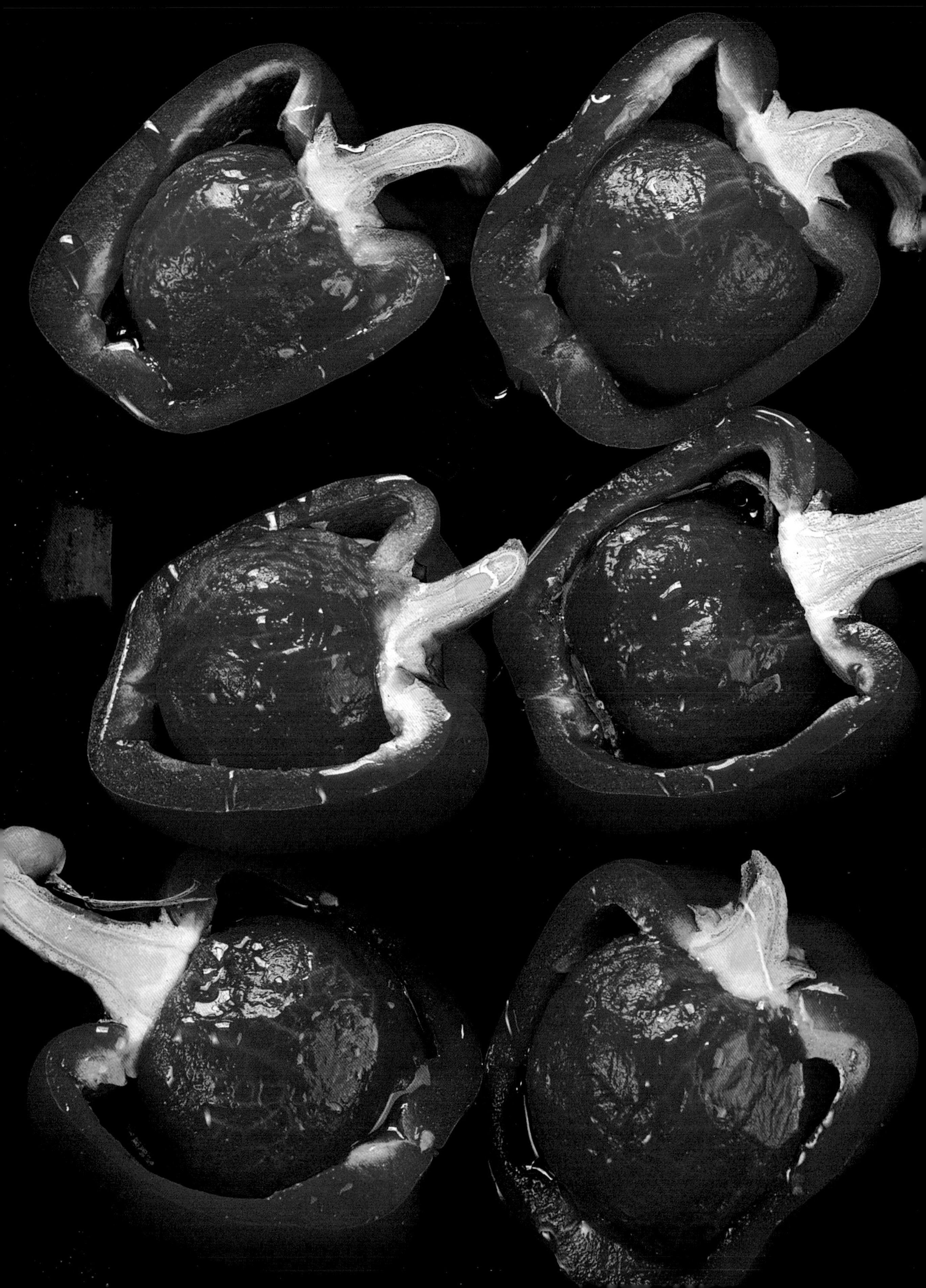

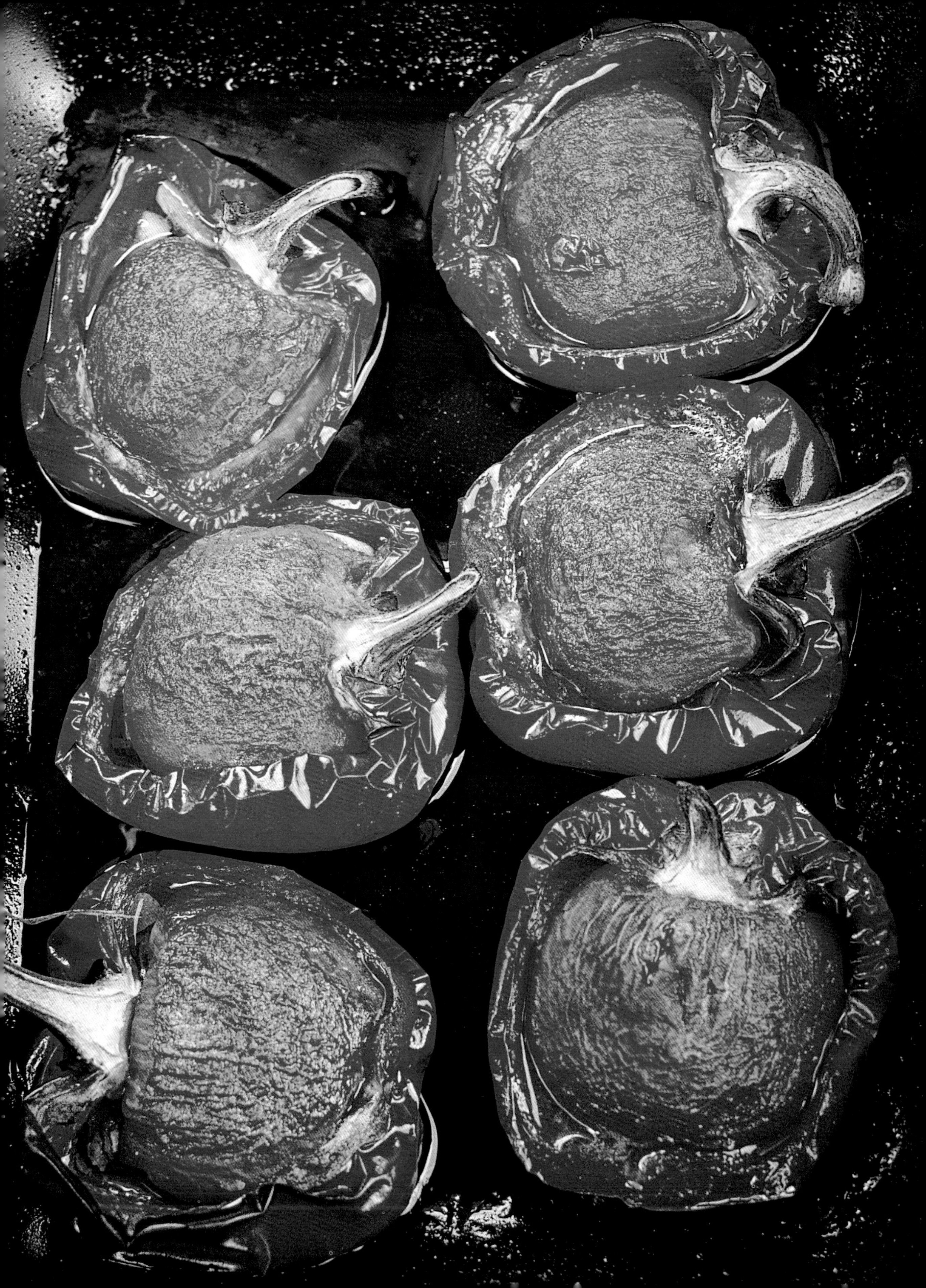

Asparagus with Hollandaise Sauce

Hollandaise is a lovely sauce that makes things like poached eggs, asparagus, poached fish or baby vegetables really luxurious. Of course it's so much better when made with really good eggs. We like to make it in an old-fashioned way – there's something deeply satisfying about stirring-in the butter, a piece at a time. The whizzing-while-pouring-on-the-melted-butter method is infallible and has plenty of devotees; it's just a matter of how much time you have.

48 stalks of asparagus
salt

For the hollandaise sauce:
2 large egg yolks
1 tablespoon white wine vinegar or tarragon vinegar
1 tablespoon water
200g butter, cut up into cubes

To make the hollandaise sauce, put the egg yolks into a heatproof bowl over a pan of barely simmering water and whisk them with the vinegar and water until they are light-coloured and a bit foamy.

Start beating in the butter, a cube at a time, not adding the next until the previous has been fully incorporated. Depending on whether you have used salted or unsalted butter, add salt to taste.

The sauce will keep warm in the basin suspended over hottish water for about 1 hour. If it splits, add a tablespoon of boiling water and whisk vigorously.

Snap off the woody base from each asparagus spear. Cook the asparagus in plenty of salted boiling water until it is just tender, about 6 to 8 minutes depending on the thickness of the stalks.

Drain the asparagus well and put the spears on warm plates straight away. Serve the sauce separately, allowing the diners to spoon it over the asparagus.

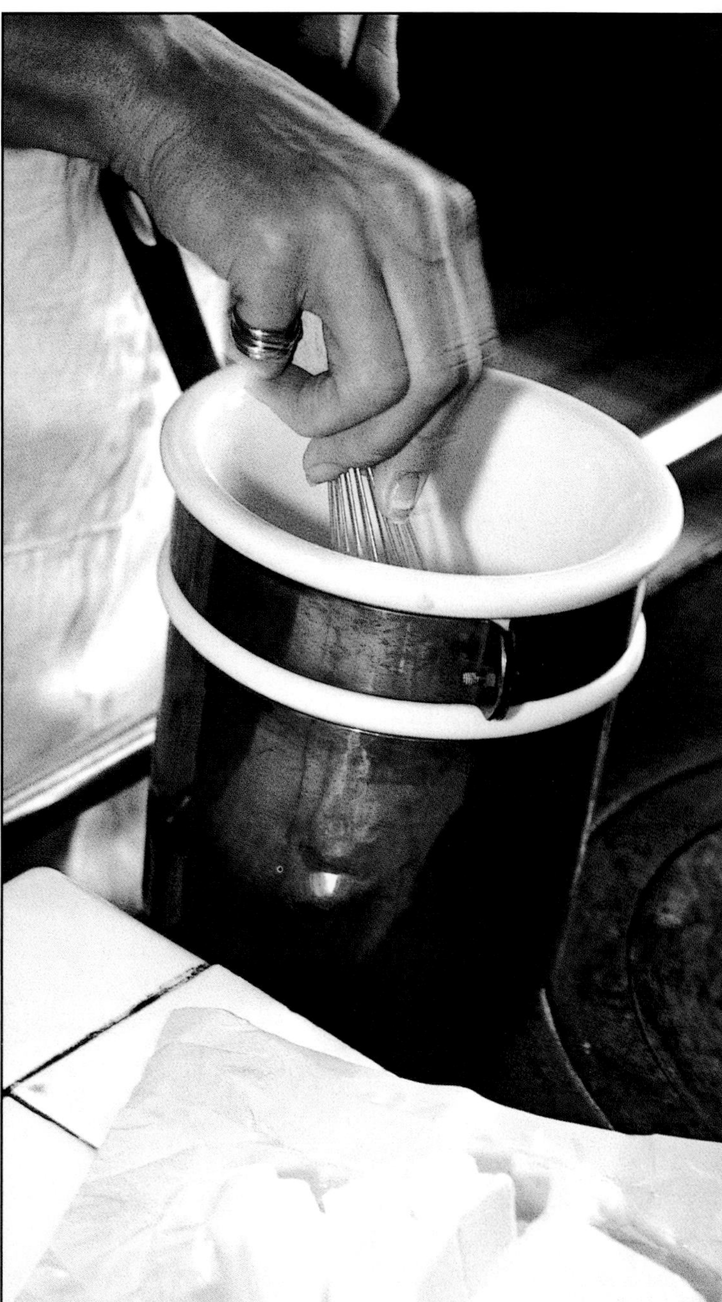

Oysters Rockefeller

A great and glamorous way to eat rock oysters for those who don't like them raw. This dish is very filling, so we always allow four oysters per person as a starter, though some of our friends (and family) can eat six.

rock salt
16 or 20 (or 24 if you're greedy) rock oysters (which, apart from being cheaper than natives, are available all year round)
500g spinach
75g butter
a splash of Pernod – or whatever pastis you have
1 teaspoon celery salt
a couple of dashes of Tabasco sauce
100g fresh breadcrumbs

Put a layer of rock salt in a roasting tin large enough to take the oysters in a single layer.

Sweat the spinach, with only the moisture clinging to the leaves, in a saucepan until it has wilted, then put it in the bowl of a food processor with the butter, Pernod, celery salt and Tabasco, and whizz until you have a smooth green purée. Put it into the fridge to firm up.

Preheat the oven to 230°C (450°F), Gas Mark 8.

Open the oysters, discarding the 'lid', and lay them in the roasting tin – the salt will keep them level.

When the spinach purée is firm, spread a spoonful over each oyster, using a palette knife to smooth them level. Sprinkle the breadcrumbs over the lot and place in the oven for 8 to 10 minutes until the breadcrumbs have turned golden and the spinach purée has started to bubble around the edges.

Serve immediately, eating the oysters with a fork and taking care not to burn your fingers on the very hot shells.

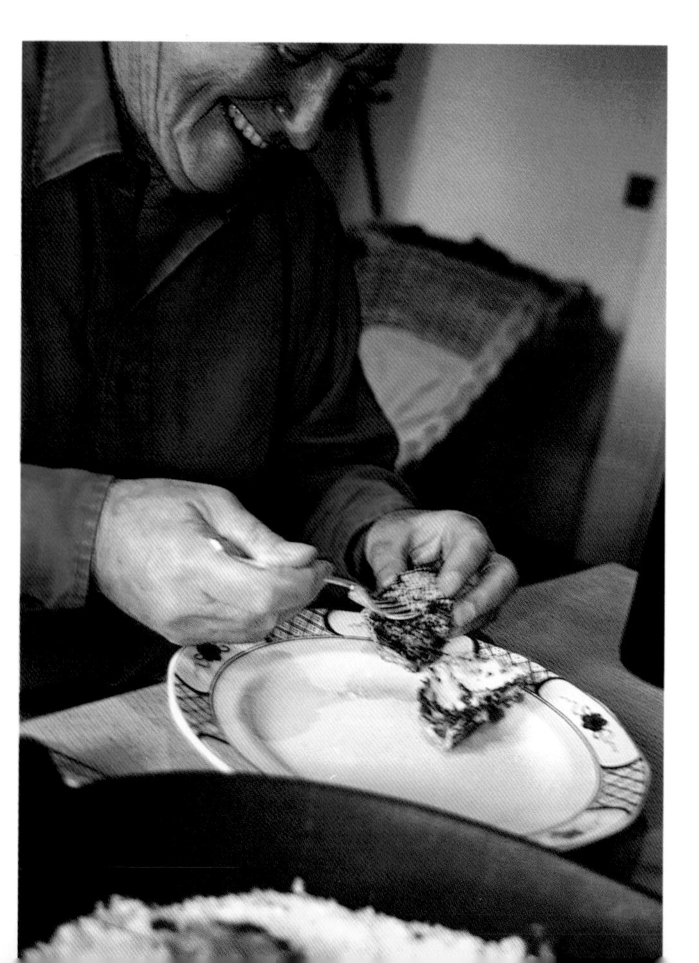

COMPAGNIE
DES
WAGONS-LITS

Main courses

Main courses generally take the principle place in a meal, indeed, a starter should whet the appetite in preparation for the main event. We think that the whole meal should be balanced. It may sound obvious but an ideal combination would not be say tomato soup followed by osso bucco with summer pudding to finish – all too tomatoey and red. Nor would a series of heavy, cream-laden courses be welcome. We once dined in one of London's more famous chef's restaurants. He insisted upon choosing our meal and sent out course after course of dishes incorporating foie gras in some form or other. While each individual dish was quite delicious and unquestionably expertly cooked, we left with our livers winching up the white flag, never wishing to ingest another morsel of foie gras ever again – a short-lived wish as it happens.

Seasonality plays its part too, in planning a meal. Warm weather makes one want to eat light and cooling dishes, salads, young vegetables and fresh herbs – all of which are readily available during summer months. Winter provides an excellent opportunity to seek out cured hams, salamis and sausages, hearty braises, game, roasts, and make the most of winter vegetables like brassicas, root vegetables and winter salads like endive.

There is also the practicality of planning your time to consider. Providing a complicated starter, followed by a main course that needs lots of attention just before you serve it will leave you too frazzled to enjoy anything yourself. Try to have a starter that requires the minimum of fuss and a main course that needs only heating up in the oven, allowing you time to cook your prepared vegetable accompaniment.

Smoked Haddock

A wonderful, comforting dish, ideally served with poached eggs and plain boiled potatoes, though champ, the savoury mash from Ireland, is a delicious alternative.

300g undyed smoked haddock, or 350g finnan haddock
milk and water – for poaching
8 really fresh eggs

Put the haddock in a shallow pan and cover with equal amounts of milk and water. Bring to a simmer and poach the fish for 10 minutes. Remove the haddock from the pan, reserving the liquid, and divide among 4 plates, keeping them warm.

Bring the reserved liquid to the boil, then, keeping it simmering, quickly break the eggs into the pan. You may need to do this in batches. Cover with a lid and carefully take the pan off the heat. Check after about 5 minutes to see if the eggs are sufficiently cooked – the yolks should be runny, but it's really a matter of taste.

Put 2 eggs on each plate and serve immediately with mashed potatoes, champ or even buttered toast.

Skate Wing with Beurre Noisette

Buy skate wings just before you are going to cook them – they need to be very fresh. There's nothing worse than skate that's gone off; the rank ammonia smell literally turns the stomach. If the wings are very large, one will probably serve two people, otherwise allow one per person.

4 skate wings, skinned, but still on the bone
80g butter
few drops of white wine vinegar
4 tablespoons capers

For the court bouillon:
1 litre water
½ glass white wine
a splash of white wine vinegar
½ onion, finely sliced
a bunch of parsley stalks
1 teaspoon black peppercorns
1 tablespoon sea salt
1 bay leaf

To make the court bouillon, put all the ingredients into a large shallow pan, bring to a simmer and allow to gently blip for about 20 minutes.

Bring the court bouillon back to a simmer, add the skate wings and poach for 10 to 12 minutes.

Meanwhile, put the butter in a small sauté pan and cook until starting to brown slightly. Swirl the pan a bit, watching it carefully, and when the bits at the bottom of the pan have achieved a really nutty brown, strain the butter into a clean pan. You can now add a few drops of vinegar and the capers.

Serve the skate wings on large hot plates, spooning over the brown butter and capers.

Plain boiled potatoes are the best accompaniment for this dish.

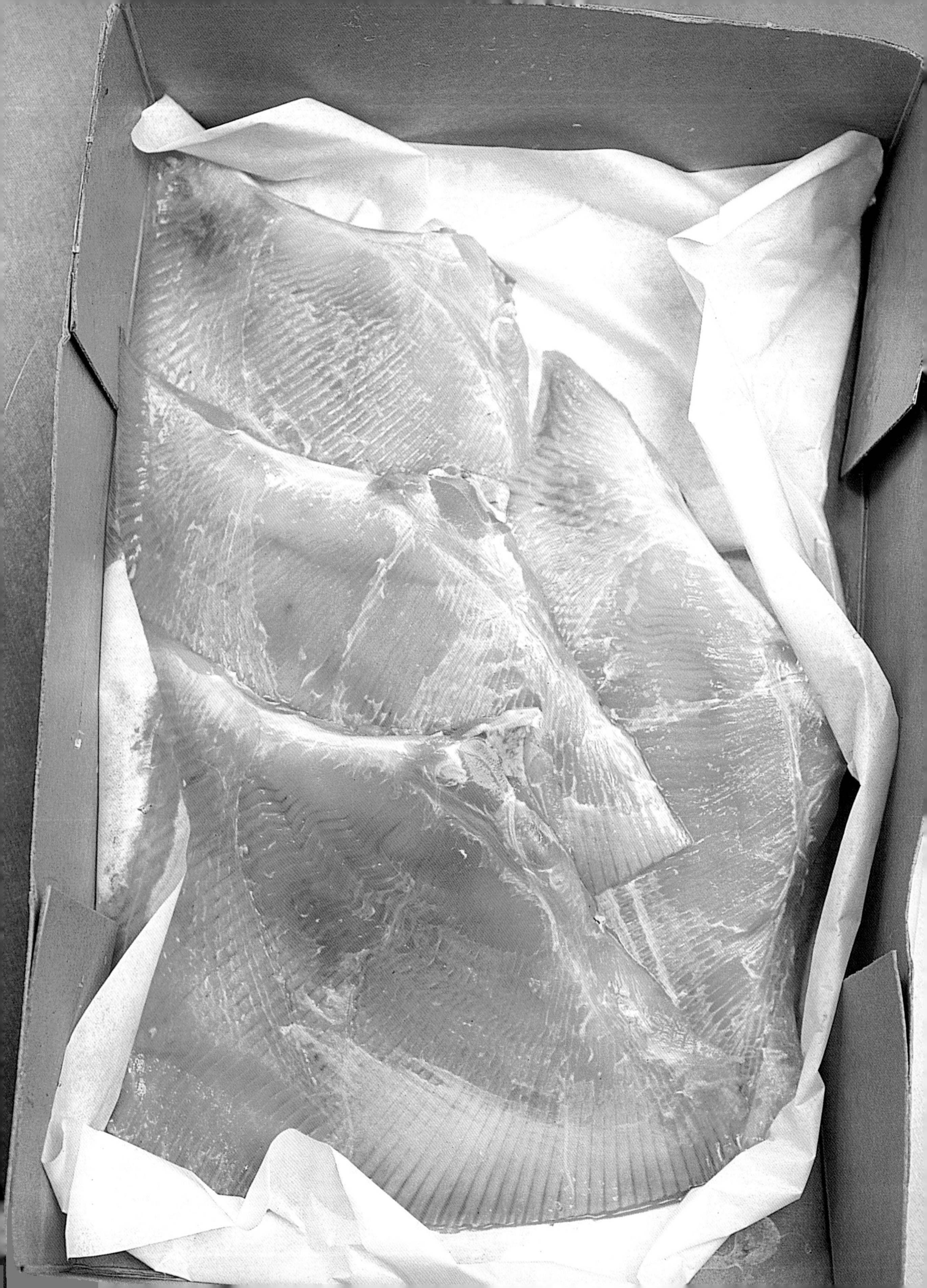

Wild Salmon with Hollandaise Sauce

Increasingly difficult to get, wild salmon has regained its luxury status. The lurid pink, farmed fish is a poor relation and generally not at all nice. The exception, however, is organically farmed salmon from the Orkney Islands, complete with Soil Association approval (one doesn't expect the Soil Association to approve things other than those grown in a garden or field but apparently the fact that these salmon are not fed with antibiotics and growth-promoting hormones, as regular farmed fish are, is good enough to qualify for organic labelling). It's a rather pretty pale pink and has a delicate flavour.

4 tablespoons plain flour
salt and white pepper
4 tablespoons clarified butter
4 wild salmon steaks, or fillet cuts, each weighing about 175g
hollandaise sauce (see page 66)
lemon halves

Mix the flour, salt and pepper together on a flat plate. Just before cooking, heat the clarified butter in a shallow sauté pan until it's very hot. Lightly dip both sides of the fish in the flour, shaking off any excess.

Put the pieces of fish in the hot pan and cook each side for about 3 minutes – it depends really on how thick the pieces are, and how cooked you like them, 3 minutes will give you a slightly rare centre to the fish, with a crusty outside.

We think broad beans, sorrel, spinach or fresh peas are the perfect accompanying vegetables, together with new potatoes. Lemon halves and hollandaise sauce complete the dish.

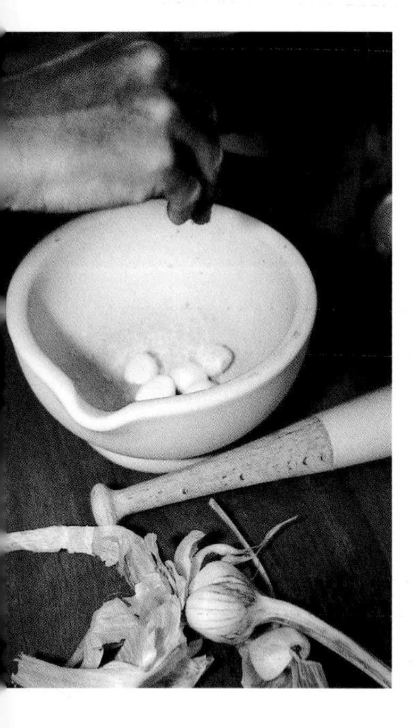

Le Grand Aïoli

Serves 6 to 8 people

1 to 1.5 kg white fish
court bouillon (see page 75)
a selection from the following vegetables, preferably very young:
artichokes, asparagus, broad beans, carrots, courgettes, French beans, kohl rabi, peas, potatoes
8 eggs
tomatoes, radishes, lettuce hearts, all halved

For the aïoli:

8 garlic cloves – preferably sweet new season's
rock salt
3 egg yolks
about 500ml olive oil – the best you can lay your hands on
a squeeze of lemon juice

Poach the fish very gently in the court bouillon until the flesh just flakes easily when tested with the tip of a knife – this should take about 10 minutes, but the time will depend on the thickness of the fish. When it is cooked, remove the skin and any bones, keeping the fish whole as much as possible. Allow to cool then place in the centre of a very large serving platter.

Meanwhile, steam or simmer the vegetables separately. Allow them to cool then arrange them around the fish.

Cook the eggs until they are not quite hard-boiled. Cool the eggs in cold water, shell and halve them, and arrange, too, on the platter, adding the tomatoes, radishes and lettuce hearts as well.

To make the aïoli, crush the garlic in a mortar with a little rock salt until it is a paste. Mix in the egg yolks and amalgamate well. Start adding the olive oil, drop by drop, until the mixture starts to thicken, then add the oil in a steady stream, as for mayonnaise. The mixture should be really thick, shiny and golden, so add only a few drops of lemon juice – you don't want to slacken it too much.

The whole dish should be at room temperature, and is really great eaten outdoors. Place the platter on the table, serve the aïoli in the mortar and let everyone help themselves. Drink some delicious chilled Provençale rosé with this.

Turbot with Beurre Blanc

One of the finest and most expensive fish, turbot is, rightly, considered a luxury. It needs little to accompany it; the quality of the fish is all. Gentle steaming or poaching in a light court bouillon is all that is required. Traditionally the accompanying sauce for pike or shad, beurre blanc is light and suits the firm white flesh of turbot.

court bouillon (see page 75)
800g fillet of turbot in 200g portions

For the beurre blanc:
6 shallots, very finely chopped
200ml white wine vinegar
200ml white wine
100ml water
200g very cold butter – cut into small cubes

To make the sauce, put the shallots, vinegar, wine and water into a small saucepan and boil until reduced to a third.

Take the pan off the heat and whisk in the pieces of butter, one at a time. Transfer to a sauceboat. The sauce will keep warm if set over a pan of hot water until needed.

Poach the turbot in the court bouillon for 5 minutes and serve on hot plates, handing the sauce separately at the table.

Beurre à la Maître d'Hôtel

This simple sauce is delicious served with grilled meat and fish.

200g butter, at room temperature
a large bunch of parsley, very finely chopped
juice of ½ lemon

Beat the butter to soften it, then add the parsley and lemon juice.

Cover with clingfilm and keep in the fridge until needed.

Scallops Provençale

Scallops Provençale is only worth making with really fresh scallops – frozen will not do, and be sure to get the scallops really brown and crusty.

12 large scallops with the corals
8 tomatoes, skinned (see page 62) and halved
salt and pepper
100g clarified butter
3 garlic cloves, finely chopped
a handful of parsley, chopped

About 1 hour before you begin to cook this dish, put the scallops on a plate lined with several sheets of kitchen paper. This will soak up any excess liquid that the scallops will leach.

Preheat the oven to 200°C (400°F), Gas Mark 6.

Put the tomatoes in a gratin dish, season with salt and pepper, and cook in the oven for about 35 minutes until they are soft.

Meanwhile, heat the clarified butter in a sauté pan until really hot and sauté the scallops until they are nicely browned. If the pan is hot enough you should be able to do this quickly so that the centre is only lightly cooked and melting.

Add the scallops to the tomatoes. At this stage you could sprinkle the dish with the garlic and parsley. Alternatively, swirl the garlic in the sauté pan with a knob of butter then spoon it and the parsley over the scallops and tomatoes, and serve.

Crab Salad

One of the best shellfish; we actually prefer it to lobster. The only thing necessary when eating crab is plenty of time, as one doesn't want to have to rush and perhaps miss out on all the little pickings. Brown bread and butter, mayonnaise and a half of lemon are the best accompaniments. If you are serving the crab as a starter, half a crab is sufficient for each person.

4 small to medium crabs

If you have bought live crabs the most humane way to deal with them is to place them in the freezer at –18°C (0°F) for about 2 hours; this makes them go into a sort of hibernation and closes down their central nervous system.

If you don't have space in your freezer, you will have to turn each crab on to its back and, taking care not to get in the way of the pincers, lift up the tail flap and insert a sharp knife into the small depression you will find there. This severs the central nervous cord, effectively and quickly killing the crab. It will appear to twitch, but this is only residual movement.

Bring a large pot of salted water to a fast boil, and fill the sink with cold water.

Drop the crabs into the fast-boiling water and cook for 15 minutes. You may have to cook them one or two at a time, depending on how large your pan is. Remove the crabs from the boiling water and plunge into the iced water to cool down quickly. Refrigerate the crabs as soon as they are cool enough. Otherwise, order the cooked crabs from your fishmonger!

Sole Meunière

Dover sole is a rare treat. Its firm flesh is tasty and delicate and needs little adornment. Simply grilled or sautéed are the best ways to enjoy this fish.

4 soles, weighing approximately 250g to 300g each
1 tablespoon plain flour
salt and white pepper
100g clarified butter
100g butter, melted
juice of 2 lemons
a handful of finely chopped parsley

Unless your fishmonger has done it for you, you will need to skin the soles. Start on the dark side, making a cut just above the tail fin. Holding the tail in one hand, pull the skin firmly towards the head in one sharp pull. Holding the fish with a tea towel helps matters hugely. Turn the fish over and do the white side from the head to tail. Keep the fish on the bone.

Lightly flour and season the soles. Heat the clarified butter in a sauté pan. Brown each sole for about 5 minutes on each side, then transfer them to a plate and keep them warm.

When all the fish have been cooked, add the butter, the lemon juice and the parsley and swirl around in the pan to heat up. Spoon over the soles.

Serve with plain boiled potatoes.

Moules à la Marinière

This classic method of cooking mussels is the basis for so many other mussel dishes and is a staple of bistro menus throughout Britain, France and the United States.

2 large shallots, finely chopped
300ml dry white wine
a splash of white wine vinegar
a sprig of thyme
a bay leaf
2kg mussels, washed and scraped, beards removed

To finish:
50g butter
a handful of finely chopped parsley
salt and pepper

Put the shallots into a large pan with the wine, vinegar, thyme and bay leaf and bring to a boil. Tip in the mussels, cover and cook over a high heat, shaking vigorously from time to time, until all the shells have opened. Take the pan off the heat and transfer the mussels to a large serving dish, throwing out any that haven't opened.

Discard the bay leaf and thyme from the cooking juices, and swirl in the butter and chopped parsley. Adjust the seasoning and pour the juices over the mussels.

Mouclade

Using the initial cooking method for Moules à la Marinière (opposite), the mussels can be incorporated into this rich and fragrant dish, perfect for lunch with a salad, or in smaller portions as a fairly substantial starter.

2kg mussels, washed and scraped, beards removed
2 large or 3 small shallots, finely chopped
300ml dry white wine
a splash of white wine vinegar
a sprig of thyme
a bay leaf

To finish:
100g butter
2 shallots, finely chopped
1 tablespoon plain flour
a large pinch of saffron
150ml double cream
a handful of finely chopped parsley
salt and white pepper

Cook the mussels with the shallots, wine, vinegar and herbs as for Moules à la Marinière (opposite). Then remove the mussels from the broth (which you should reserve) and take them from the shells; throw away any that are unopened. Place the mussels in a shallow 1.5-litre gratin dish.

To finish the dish, melt the butter in a small pan and sweat the shallots until soft and transparent, not browned. Stir in the flour and cook a little, making a roux. While it is bubbling, add a ladleful or two of the mussel broth, together with the saffron threads, stirring vigorously. The sauce will be rather thick, so stir in the cream and if it is still too thick, a little more broth or cream. Add the parsley, taste and add salt if necessary, and some white pepper.

Preheat the oven to 230°C (450°F), Gas Mark 8.

Spoon over the sauce over the mussels and put into the oven, or under a very hot grill, for about 5 to 8 minutes until bubbling and just burnished on top.

Crayfish

Our rivers and streams are stiff with crayfish – many fisheries regard them as a menace – yet they are comparatively difficult to get your hands on. You can order them from a good fishmonger, or if you know of a local fishery you may be able to get the keeper to bait a net for you. The crayfish must be purged for a couple of days to eliminate the gut. They are best served just boiled with mayonnaise. Crayfish bisque, made with the shells, is delicious. One of the very best things we have ever eaten was a gratin of crayfish at Paul Bocuse's eponymous restaurant just outside Lyon – one of those restaurants that is really worth the detour.

allow 6 to 8 crayfish per person
a large bunch of dill
50g salt
mayonnaise (see page 49), to serve

Put a large pan of water on to boil. Add the salt and, when it is at a full rolling boil, add the crayfish and dill. Cook the crayfish for about 5 minutes, until their shells turn bright scarlet.

Meanwhile, fill the sink with crushed ice and cold water. Remove the crayfish from the pan and transfer them to the sink to cool. Serve with mayonnaise.

Drink very chilled aquavit with lager chasers for the full Scandinavian effect.

As well as being the day the grouse shooting season starts in Britain, 12th August is the day that the krefte *(crayfish) season starts in Sweden. The parties given to celebrate the occasion are the stuff of legend – mountains of crayfish and massive quantities of beer and aquavit leading inevitably to excesses of a more corporal nature... the imagination runs wild. Quite a different story from the serious respectability of the grouse shoots.*

Brandade de Morue

One of the amazing things about the Mediterranean is that nearly every country bordering it has a repertoire of recipes involving dried salt cod, which comes all the way from Norway or Iceland. Perhaps it is a relic of the Roman Catholic fast days precluding the eating of meat. The best places to buy salt cod are usually shops selling Spanish or Portuguese specialities. This recipe is the classic dish as found in Nîmes. The salt cod needs de-salting before cooking. You can do this by soaking it in several changes of cold water, or, if feasible, under a running tap. Whichever method, it will need to be soaked for at least eighteen hours, preferably twenty-four, after which it will be ready for cooking.

1 onion, finely chopped
½ teaspoon black peppercorns
1 bay leaf
500g salt cod
500ml olive oil, warmed
1 fat garlic clove, crushed
120ml single cream, warmed
salt and white pepper

Half-fill a pan with water, add the onion, peppercorns and bay leaf and simmer for 15 minutes. Add the salt cod, return to the boil, then remove from the heat and allow the fish to stand in the hot water for 10 minutes.

Lift the salt cod out of the pan and remove any skin and bones. Discard the water and flavourings.

Heat 100ml of the olive oil with the garlic in a clean saucepan, and then add the cod. Mash the cod to a paste, keeping the heat very gentle indeed. While stirring and mashing vigorously, gradually add the remaining warmed oil, alternating it with the warmed cream. The mixture must be really smooth and white. Taste and add salt and white pepper to taste.

Brandade is served tepid, with slices of baguette that have been lightly fried in olive oil. It is a deeply comforting dish and might even encourage one to have spiritual thoughts.

Fish Pie

Perennially popular, the comforting simplicity belies the amount of work – and pans – this staple of the nursery involves. Make the pie well in advance, allowing the cooking smells to disappear completely before you eat. The recipe can easily be doubled up to serve more – it actually seems to improve the larger you make it!

a few parsley stalks
½ onion, sliced
1 bay leaf
700ml milk
250ml water
800g white fish, about half of which should be undyed smoked haddock
60g butter
60g plain flour
a handful of chopped parsley
1 tablespoon anchovy essence
4 hard-boiled eggs, shelled and coarsely chopped
250g peeled prawns
pepper

For the mashed potato:
750g potatoes, cut into pieces
50g butter
300ml milk

To make the mashed potato, boil the potatoes in lightly salted water until tender. Drain, then cover with a tea towel to dry out a bit. Melt the butter in the potato pan with half the milk. Press the potatoes through a ricer, or push through the finest blade of a mouli-legumes into the butter and milk mixture and mix thoroughly. Add more milk until the mash reaches the consistency you like.

Put the parsley stalks, the sliced onion and the bay leaf in a shallow pan with the 700 ml milk and 250ml water, then bring to the boil. Reduce to a simmer, add the fish and poach for 10 minutes until just cooked. Using a slotted spoon, lift the fish from the liquid. Remove the skin and bones, and flake the fish into a gratin dish. Reserve the liquid.

Melt the butter in a large saucepan, then add the flour and cook a little, stirring with a wooden spoon. Pour about 700ml of the reserved liquid through a strainer into the pan, stirring all the time to make a sauce the consistency of double cream. Add the chopped parsley, anchovy essence, eggs and prawns. Taste the sauce and add some pepper (it is unlikely you will need any salt) and pour over the flaked fish. Shake the dish gently to distribute the sauce evenly and top with the mashed potato.

If you want to keep the pie for a while before you bake it, keep it in the fridge, but take it out at least 1 hour before cooking.

Preheat the oven to 200°C (400°F), Gas Mark 6. Put the fish pie into the oven for 35 to 40 minutes until it is browned on top and bubbling round the edges.

We always seem to eat this with peas – fresh in summer, frozen petits pois in winter.

Fish Cakes

Fish fingers for grown-ups. These fish cakes can be made using white fish, smoked fish or for real luxury, salmon.

3 large baking potatoes
500g cooked fish, skinned and flaked
2 tablespoons finely chopped parsley
1 tablespoon anchovy essence
a squeeze of lemon juice
30g butter
salt and white pepper
1 egg, lightly beaten
2 tablespoons plain flour
1–2 tablespoons clarified butter, or oil
2 lemons, halved, to serve

Preheat the oven to 200°C (400°F), Gas Mark 6. Bake the potatoes for at least 1 hour, until they are cooked through. Take the skins off and mash the potato.

In a bowl, mix the flaked fish, chopped parsley, anchovy essence, lemon juice, butter, salt and white pepper together. Then stir in enough of the beaten egg to make a firm dough.

With floured hands make the fish cakes – either 4 big fat ones, or 8 dainty little ones. Put the cakes in the fridge for at least 30 minutes.

Lightly coat the fish cakes in flour and fry them in the clarified butter or oil until golden. Serve at once with lemon halves.

You could also serve tomato sauce, or sorrel sauce, which goes particularly well with salmon fishcakes.

Entrecôte Béarnaise

The classic of the Parisian bistro, a nice thin entrecôte steak, grilled and served with frites and béarnaise sauce, is always a popular meal. At home, we rarely cook pommes frites, generally preferring sautéed potatoes in their place. Béarnaise sauce is awfully good with other grilled meats like kidneys or lamb chops.

1 tablespoon clarified butter
4 entrecôte steaks, each weighing 200g to 250g
salt and pepper

For the béarnaise sauce:
a large bunch of tarragon
2 shallots, very finely chopped
100ml white wine
100ml tarragon vinegar
2 egg yolks
250g butter, cut into cubes

To make the béarnaise sauce, remove the top tender leaves from the tarragon stalks and reserve them. Chop the remaining leaves and the stalks and put them into a small saucepan with the shallots, white wine and vinegar. Simmer until reduced to about a tablespoonful.

Strain the liquid into a clean basin suspended over simmering water. Add the egg yolks, whisking until the mixture thickens slightly. Keeping the heat very gentle, whisk in the butter, a piece at a time until the sauce is very thick.

Chop the reserved tarragon and add to the sauce. Taste and add salt if you think it needs it. Turn off the heat.

You can keep the béarnaise sauce warm for some time in the basin suspended over hot water.

To cook the steaks, heat the clarified butter in a frying pan until really hot. Season the steaks with salt and pepper and sauté in the hot butter, cooking them for about 3 to 5 minutes on each side depending on their thickness and how well you like them done.

Transfer the cooked steaks onto hot plates and allow them to rest for a further 3 to 5 minutes before serving them with the warm béarnaise sauce.

If you are in a bit of a hurry, Beurre à la Maître d'Hôtel (page 82) is quicker to make than Béarnaise Sauce and is just as delicious for a change.

Onglet aux Echalotes

The most difficult part of this recipe is getting the onglet, or skirt as it's known in English, of beef. It is full of flavour and relatively inexpensive. A good butcher will have it (if it hasn't already been bought by the chefs in the area), and should have hung it well and removed all the connective tissue, membranes and skin. Because onglet has relatively little fat, it should be cooked quickly, rare, otherwise it will become rather tough and dry.

700g to 800g onglet – allow about 175 to 200g per person
100g clarified butter
12–16 shallots, chopped
1 wineglass of white wine
salt and pepper
a large splash of wine vinegar – we use tarragon
a large handful of parsley, chopped

Score the onglet in criss-cross fashion on both sides, cutting almost through the long muscles of the meat.

Heat half the butter in a heavy frying pan until it is really hot – almost smoking. Cook the steaks very quickly – about 1 minute each side. The idea is to get the meat really well cooked on the outside, still rare and bloody in the centre. Take the steaks out of the pan and allow them to rest, keeping them warm, while you cook the shallots.

Put the remaining butter in the pan and allow it to heat up. Throw in the shallots and cook them gently until they are golden and just starting to melt. Stir in the white wine, some salt and pepper and a splash of vinegar, scraping the pan to deglaze it. At the last moment add the parsley.

Serve the steaks on very hot plates, spooning the shallots over.

Braised Oxtail

Really cold weather always inspires thoughts of hearty stews, and oxtail ranks amongst the best of winter dishes. As with most braises, this is best made the day before you want to eat it, firstly to allow you to remove the rather large amount of fat with ease, and secondly, and probably more importantly, to let the flavours develop and deepen. Braised oxtail is delicious with large quantities of fluffy mashed potato, or parsnip purée, and something sharp like red cabbage.

2 carrots
2 onions
2 sticks of celery
a knob of butter
a knob of dripping
2 tablespoons flour
salt and pepper
2 oxtails, cut up
1 wineglass of red wine
2 x 400g cans of peeled tomatoes
1 tablespoon bitter orange marmalade
thinly pared rind of 1 orange

Preheat the oven to 140°C (275°F), Gas Mark 1. Finely chop the carrots, onions and celery in a food processor.

Melt the butter in a large flameproof casserole. Add the chopped vegetables and sauté gently without colouring, stirring from time to time.

Meanwhile, melt the dripping in the largest frying pan you have. Season the flour with salt and pepper and put it in a large polythene bag with the oxtail, a few pieces at a time, shaking the bag vigorously to give the oxtail a fine coating of flour. Fry the meat in batches in the dripping until it is well browned, placing the cooked pieces in the casserole with the vegetables.

When all the oxtail has been browned, tip the fat from the frying pan, return the pan to the heat and add the wine, the tomatoes, and the marmalade. Bring to the boil, scraping the bits from the bottom of the pan. Allow the wine to reduce and thicken slightly then pour over the meat and vegetables in the casserole. Put on a tight-fitting lid, place in the oven and cook for 2½ to 3 hours – the meat should be virtually falling off the bone.

Remove the casserole from the oven and leave in a cool place to get really cold. The next day you will be able to take the solidified fat off the jellied juices very easily.

To serve, warm the casserole slowly over a gentle heat, add the orange rind and salt and pepper to taste. Allow the stew to heat through thoroughly – this will take about 30 minutes. Stir occasionally to prevent sticking.

Serve on very hot plates with lots of mashed potato.

Steak and Kidney Pudding

A legendary dish of olde England. In days gone by, oysters were used to make the more expensive beef stretch further, nowadays the addition of oysters is a luxury. Traditionally, the raw filling was put into the suet paste and steamed. We cook the filling separately, allow it to cool and then fill the pudding. If you are using oysters, you can add them to the cooked filling, or poach them and serve them on the side.

75g beef dripping or butter
1 large onion, coarsely chopped
1kg stewing steak, cubed
350ml beef stock (see page 246)
1 teaspoon mushroom ketchup
1 teaspoon Worcestershire sauce
200ml red wine
1 teaspoon anchovy essence
450g ox kidney, cored and cut into cubes

For the suet pastry:
300g self-raising flour
½ teaspoon salt
½ teaspoon white pepper
120g suet
iced water

Melt the dripping or butter in a large flameproof casserole, add the onion and brown it in the fat. Remove the onion and set aside, then brown the steak in batches, then remove to rest with the onions.

Pour off the fat from the casserole and put the pan back on the heat, adding the stock, mushroom ketchup, Worcestershire sauce, wine, and anchovy essence. Bring to a simmer, scraping up the bits in the pan. Return the onion and meat to the casserole and add the kidney. Cover the casserole and allow to barely simmer for about 1½ hours. Or place it in a preheated oven, 140°C (275°F), Gas Mark 1. Remove the casserole from the oven and allow to cool completely, overnight if possible.

Make the pastry at least 4 hours before you want to eat. Put the flour, salt, pepper and suet in a large basin and mix. Add enough iced water to make a soft, but not too floppy dough. Press it out into a large circle, cut out a quarter section and use the larger piece of dough to line a buttered 2 litre pudding basin.

Fill the lined basin with the cold meat mixture, adding enough gravy to fill the bowl to within 2cm of the top. Dampen the edges of the pastry and use the remaining pastry to cover the basin. Tie a sheet of buttered, pleated greaseproof paper over the top of the basin, then do the same with a piece of kitchen foil.

Fill a large pan with enough water to come at least half-way up the sides of the basin. Bring the water to a boil, then lower the basin in, cover and keep the water at a rolling boil for about 10 minutes. Lower the heat to keep the water boiling and continue to cook for 2½ to 3 hours. Top up the boiling water when necessary.

Remove the basin from the water, tie a large napkin around it and serve.

Daube de Boeuf

Like many slow braises, this is better made the day before you want to eat it.

2 tablespoons beef dripping
500g onions, sliced
800g to 900g rump beef, cut into large slices
boiling water
4 garlic cloves
a handful of finely chopped parsley
8 to 10 salted anchovy fillets
3 tablespoons red wine vinegar
salt and pepper

Preheat the oven to 160°C (325°F), Gas Mark 3.

Melt half the dripping in a large flameproof casserole and cook the onions slowly until they are soft and brown – this will take 20 to 30 minutes.

Meanwhile, melt the remaining dripping in a frying pan and fry the slices of beef in batches until they are nicely browned. Add the beef to the onions in the casserole and pour in enough boiling water to just cover the meat.

Cover with a lid, put into the oven and braise for about 1 to 1½ hours until the meat is tender.

Just before serving, very finely chop the garlic, parsley and anchovies together and stir into the casserole with the red wine vinegar. At this stage taste and add salt and pepper as needed.

This is delicious with plain boiled potatoes and braised carrots. A salad of Little Gem or butterhead lettuces is marvellous with the braised jus – it needs no other dressing.

Roast Beef

Few people can resist the sight and smell of roast standing ribs of beef and eye-watering horseradish sauce. Buy the best beef you can, organic Scotch, Black Angus or Hereford, from a really good butcher. It will have been properly hung and have an ample amount of fat – essential for flavour and texture. Look for really dark, almost burgundy meat with creamy yellow fat. Allow one rib for two to three people, depending on how greedy they are, and ask the butcher for the trimmings.

Serves 6–8

2kg to 3kg beef on the bone, with trimmings
salt and pepper

For the gravy:

1 wineglass of red wine
1 onion, roughly chopped
1 carrot, roughly chopped
1 stick of celery, roughly chopped
a few parsley stalks
a few dried porcini mushrooms, soaked for 15 minutes in a bowl of warm water
a dash of anchovy essence

Preheat the oven to about 220°C (425°F), Gas Mark 7.

Put the beef in a roasting tin and press salt and pepper into the fat. Put the beef trimmings in the pan, too. Place the beef in the oven and cook it for about 15 minutes per 450g if you like it rare; 20 minutes per 450g for medium; or 25 minutes per 450g for well done. After about 20 minutes, take out the browned trimmings.

In a small saucepan, bring the wine to a boil, put a lit match to it and let it flame until the fire dies down. Add the trimmings, onion, carrot, celery, parsley stalks and the soaked mushrooms and their soaking water. Bring to the boil and simmer for about 1 hour, adding water if the liquid reduces too much.

When the beef is cooked, transfer it to a platter or board and cover it with kitchen foil to keep it warm. It is best to leave it for at least 20 minutes, to allow the meat to rest.

Strain the fat off the roasting tin into a bowl – this precious dripping is really worth keeping for roasting potatoes or spreading on toast.

Put the roasting tin on the heat, adding the contents of the small pan. Scrape up the bits clinging to the pan and squash the vegetables into the liquid as it comes to the boil. Pour the gravy through a conical strainer into a clean pan and add salt, pepper and a splash of anchovy essence to taste, then reheat and serve with the carved beef.

Shepherd's Pie

Or is it cottage pie? We always think of it being shepherd's pie when made with roast lamb, cottage pie when made with beef. It's almost worth roasting too large a joint of lamb to have enough left over for shepherd's pie the next day. The pie can always be made from scratch, using minced lamb, but there's something deeply satisfying about the dish made with roast leftovers.

1 tablespoon dripping or oil
500g cold roast lamb, including some skin and fatty parts, roughly chopped
1 carrot, finely chopped
1 stick of celery, finely chopped
1 large onion, finely chopped
250ml lamb or vegetable stock, or left-over gravy
a squeeze of tomato purée
1 tablespoon anchovy essence
salt and pepper
1.5kg potatoes, peeled and cubed
200ml hot milk
60g butter

Preheat the oven to 180°C (350°F), Gas Mark 4.

Heat the dripping or oil in a large frying pan and sauté the meat and vegetables until nicely browned. Add the stock or gravy, tomato purée and anchovy essence and simmer, adding salt and pepper to taste. Cook gently for about 15 minutes and transfer into a gratin dish.

Meanwhile, boil the potatoes in salted water until soft. Drain them, return them to the pan and cover with a tea towel for 5 minutes. Mash the potatoes, or push them through a ricer, add some of the hot milk and butter and mix, adding more milk until you have the consistency you like.

Carefully spoon the potato over the meat in the gratin dish and either smooth the top or rake it into furrows with a fork, depending on how you like it. Bake it in the oven for about 30 minutes. Turn the heat up towards the end of the cooking, or put the dish under the grill, to brown the top.

Boudin Noir Parmentier

A sort of French shepherd's pie. It must be French boudins noir – while we have a great liking for the black pudding from Bury, Lancashire it just does not work in the same way. And we like to eat it with very foamy mashed potatoes.

750 g potatoes, cut into pieces
75g butter
2 boudins noirs, thickly sliced
300ml milk
salt

Preheat the oven to 200°C (400°F), Gas Mark 6.

Put the potatoes on to cook in lightly salted water and boil until just tender. Melt 25g of the butter in a frying pan, and sauté the boudins noirs in the pan; they will tend to fall apart a bit but it doesn't matter. When they are done, put them into the bottom of a gratin dish.

Drain the cooked potatoes in a colander, then cover with a clean tea towel to dry out a bit. Melt the remaining butter in the potato saucepan with half the milk – it's important that the milk is really hot when making mashed potato. Push the potatoes through the finest blade of a mouli-legumes, or press through a ricer into the butter and milk mixture and incorporate thoroughly. Depending on the type of potatoes and how foamy you like your mash, add more milk until it reaches the consistency you like, then pile it on the boudins.

Put the dish into the oven 15 minutes to gild the top.

Serve with something spicy and sharp – red cabbage or a green salad.

Boeuf à la Mode or Braised Beef with Carrots

2 tablespoons dripping or oil
1.5kg braising beef – rump or topside
100g each of carrots, onions and celery, finely sliced
1 calf's foot
1 bay leaf
a sprig of parsley
a sprig of thyme
500ml beef stock (see page 246) or water/stock combination
400g carrots, sliced lengthways if large
salt and pepper
a splash of Madeira or port
a small handful of chopped parsley

Preheat the oven to 150°C (300°F), Gas Mark 2.

Heat the dripping or oil in a large lidded casserole, add the beef and cook until brown and crusty on the outside. Spoon out most of the fat; add the finely sliced vegetables, calf's foot, herbs and stock.

Bring to a simmer on top of the stove. Cover, then transfer to the oven and braise for 1½ hours.

Meanwhile, cook the 400g carrots in a pan of lightly salted boiling water for 10–15 minutes until just tender. Drain well and keep warm.

Remove the beef from the casserole, cover and keep warm. Take the calf's foot out (delicious pickings for later). Skim the fat from the braising juices and strain through a conical sieve into a clean pan that you can bring to the table. Add salt, pepper and a splash of Madeira or port.

Slice the beef, return it and the boiled carrots to the dish and, making sure that it is really hot, serve sprinkled with some chopped parsley.

Plain boiled potatoes are an excellent accompaniment, as are young carrots or a green salad.

Boeuf à la Mode en Gelée

During the summer the braised beef can be delicious served cold, in which case the juices set into a flavoursome jelly. You can clear the juices after skimming off all the fat, by adding a couple of egg whites and allowing it to simmer for 20 minutes. You will then be able to lift off the foamy scum. Strain the now clear stock though a couple of layers of muslin. Slice the beef and arrange on a shallow dish with the carrots and ladle over the clear juices, cool to room temperature then allow to set in the fridge for a couple of hours.

Blanquette de Veau

This can be an extraordinarily good dish. Albert Roux (chef-patron of the Michelin 3-starred restaurant in London, Le Gavroche), who prepared it once for us, says that the secret lies in the quality of the veal and the cream.

700g veal from the shoulder
or best end, cubed
1 onion
2 cloves
2 carrots, chopped
2 leeks, chopped
1 stick of celery, chopped
bouquet garni – parsley stalks,
sprigs of thyme and a bay leaf
salt and white pepper
juice of 1 lemon
20 shallots
50g butter
150g white mushrooms
120ml cream
2 egg yolks
handful finely chopped parsley

Put the veal into a large flameproof casserole, add the onion stuck with the cloves, the carrots, leeks, celery, bouquet garni, white pepper, lemon juice and enough water to cover. Bring to a gentle simmer, skimming off any scum. Allow to cook very gently for 1½ hours. Transfer the pieces of meat to a clean pan.

Gently fry the shallots in half the butter in a shallow sauté pan without colouring, then add them to the veal.

Cook the mushrooms in the same butter, in a similar way, and add them to the meat.

Add the rest of the butter and the cream to the sauté pan, and simmer to thicken slightly. Add salt to taste.

Just before serving, beat the egg yolks in a small basin, heat the cream and butter to just below simmering and add a spoonful of the cream to the egg yolks, whisking carefully. Take the pan off the heat and add the egg mixture to the cream. Tip this on to the veal and fold it together.

To serve, strew the blanquette with finely chopped parsley and serve with plainly boiled rice.

Grilled Veal Kidneys

Plainly grilled and served with Anchovy Butter (see below) or Beurre à la Maître d'Hôtel (see page 82), veal kidney is one of the simplest and most delicious of offal dishes. Try to get the kidney wrapped in its blanket of suet; the suet freezes well and is sublime finely chopped and used in the making of suetcrust pastry.

2 veal kidneys
salt and pepper
a small piece of the suet or 1 tablespoon clarified butter

Split each kidney in two lengthways and sprinkle with salt and pepper.

Melt the suet or heat the butter in a sauté pan and quickly fry the kidneys – they are nicer if browned on the outside and still a little rosy within.

Serve the kidneys immediately on very hot plates with some anchovy butter or beurre à la maître d'hôtel.

Sautéed potatoes (see page 171) and a green vegetable complete the meal.

Veal Chops with Anchovy Butter

The excellent anchovy butter used in this dish is also wonderful with grilled meats, fish, boiled eggs or just spread on toast.

1 tablespoon clarified butter
4 veal chops
watercress, to serve

For the anchovy butter:
50g anchovy fillets, salted and packed in oil, drained
100g butter, softened
a squeeze of lemon juice

To make the anchovy butter, pound the anchovies in a sturdy bowl – a mortar is ideal – until they turn to paste. Add the butter and work into the anchovies, adding a squeeze of lemon juice.

If you want a fine finish, you can push the anchovy butter through a sieve, then pack it into a bowl and chill until you need it. We rarely bother to sieve it, rather liking the odd fishy-salty solid.

Heat the clarified butter in a frying pan until it is really hot. Fry the chops on one side for about 5 minutes until they are really golden brown, then on the other side, which will probably need 3 minutes.

Allow the veal chops to rest in a warm place for about 5 minutes, then transfer them onto hot plates and serve them accompanied by a bunch of watercress and a pat of anchovy butter.

Osso Bucco

Osso bucco is traditionally served with risotto alla Milanese, though we tend to prefer buttered tagliatelle – but whichever accompaniment you choose, one essential is gremolata to sprinkle over the finished dish. You won't need marrow spoons to scoop out the delicious marrow – it comes out quite easily with the help of a rounded knife blade.

4–6 slices of shin of veal, including marrow
1 tablespoon flour
salt and pepper
50g butter
1 tablespoon olive oil
2 onions, very finely chopped
2 carrots, finely chopped
2 sticks of celery, finely chopped
1 clove garlic, minced
1 glass of white wine
400g can of tomatoes
a sprig of oregano
a sprig of thyme
veal stock – optional

For the gremolata:
a handful of parsley
2 fat garlic cloves
grated rind of 1 lemon

Preheat the oven to 180°C (350°F), Gas Mark 4.

To make the gremolata, chop the parsley, garlic and lemon rind together, inhaling the wonderful aroma. Set aside in a small serving bowl.

Season the flour with salt and pepper. Put it in a large plastic bag with the slices of veal and give them a good shake.

Heat up half the butter and the olive oil in a frying pan and when really hot add the veal in a single layer – you may have to do this in two batches, depending on how large your frying pan is.

Meanwhile, melt the remaining butter in a large, lidded, flameproof casserole and gently sauté the vegetables and garlic.

When the veal is brown on both sides, transfer it to the casserole and place on top of the vegetables. When you have cooked all the veal slices, tip out most of the fat from the frying pan, and pour in the wine, bringing it to a boil while scraping up the bits in the pan.

Add the tomatoes, break them up in the liquid, then add the oregano and thyme. Pour onto the veal in the casserole. You may need to add some stock to bring the liquid level to the top of the veal. Put the lid on and cook in the oven for 2 hours. Check occasionally to ensure the casserole does not dry out. If it is, add a little more stock. It is cooked when the meat is very tender, almost falling off the bone.

Serve accompanied by the gremolata in a bowl for diners to sprinkle upon their osso bucco.

Cassoulet

This is a dish that comes with a great pedigree, the three main sources of the dish, Castelnaudary, Carcassonne and Toulouse, being known as 'la Trinité'. This recipe follows none of the strictures laid down by these cities, but rather takes its lead from a combination of all three. We always make it for a lunch after Christmas with the goose stock and any goose left-overs.

Serves 8 to 10

1.5kg pork belly – get the butcher to remove the rind, but be sure to keep it
4 tablespoons goose fat
1kg white haricot beans, soaked in cold water for 12 hours, drained
12 garlic cloves, bruised
2 onions, halved and stuck with 4 cloves
2 bay leaves
a large sprig of thyme
400g can of tomatoes
stock – optional
1 boned, rolled 1.5 kg shoulder of lamb
1kg Toulouse sausages
salt and pepper
8 to 10 pieces of preserved goose or duck
fresh breadcrumbs

Preheat the oven to 180°C (350°F), Gas Mark 4.

Cut the pork belly into thick slices and the rind into small squares.

Melt the goose fat in a large flameproof casserole and gently sauté the belly and rind. Add the beans together with the garlic, onions, bay leaves, thyme and the tomatoes. Pour in enough water or stock to cover by at least 3cm, cover with a lid and cook very gently for 2 hours.

Meanwhile, put the shoulder of lamb in a roasting tin and cook in the oven for 1 hour. During the final 20 minutes add the Toulouse sausages to the roasting tin and brown them in the oven with the lamb. Allow the lamb to rest for about 10 minutes then carve it into thick slices.

When the beans have cooked, add the preserved goose or duck, the sliced lamb, the sausages and season with salt and pepper. The casserole should be neither wet nor dry – *fondant* is the desired consistency, so if you think it is too dry add a little stock.

Cover the top of the cassoulet with a thick layer of breadcrumbs, which will soak up the slightly alarming quantity of fat on the surface, and place in the oven for 15 minutes.

Take the casserole from the oven and, with the back of a spoon, push the breadcrumb crust back into the beans and meat, and return the dish to the oven. Repeat this process of sinking the breadcrumbs a few more times – seven times for a proper Castelnaudary finish, eight for the Toulouse version – until a thick crust has formed.

Store the cassoulet in the larder and reheat it when you are really hungry.

Ham Saupiquet

A real Burgundian dish, incorporating all the elements of the Morvan district – ham, shallots, wine, vinegar and cream.

2 tablespoons butter
300g cooked ham, sliced
6 shallots, finely sliced
2 garlic cloves, finely sliced
50ml red wine
30ml red wine vinegar
1 tablespoon juniper berries
150ml double cream
a sprig of thyme
salt and pepper

Preheat the oven to 200°C (400°F), Gas Mark 6.

Heat the butter in a frying pan, sauté the ham until lightly browned and transfer to a gratin dish.

Gently fry the shallots and garlic in the butter until softened and golden.

Meanwhile, put the wine and vinegar into a small saucepan with the juniper berries and reduce to 2 tablespoons. Add to the shallots, together with the cream, thyme and salt and pepper. Simmer gently until thickened, then spoon over the ham in the gratin dish. Put the dish in the oven for about 10 to 15 minutes until golden.

Toulouse Sausages with Lentils

Toulouse sausages are made from coarsely ground pork; flavoured with garlic and herbs they are generally rather substantial.

250g smoked bacon, cubed into lardons
200g Puy lentils
1 onion, halved and stuck with 2 cloves
a bay leaf
a sprig of thyme
1 garlic clove, crushed
a squeeze of tomato purée
1 litre chicken stock (see page 247) or vegetable stock (see page 246)
8 Toulouse sausages

Preheat the oven to 200°C (400°F), Gas Mark 6.

Gently sauté the bacon in a casserole until just turning crisp. Add the lentils, onion, bay leaf, thyme, garlic, tomato purée and stock. Heat gently and simmer for 20 minutes.

Meanwhile, put the Toulouse sausages in a roasting tin and bake in the oven for about 20 minutes until they are nicely browned all over.

Add the sausages to the lentils and return to a simmer for 10 minutes.

Serve with crusty baguette and a sharply dressed green salad.

Gammon with Parsley Sauce

This recipe is more than enough for 4 people; however, the left-over gammon is never wasted, making excellent ham sandwiches spread with plenty of English mustard or pickle.

Serves 4 with left-overs, or 6 at one sitting

a piece of gammon weighing about 1.5kg
small bunch of parsley
small bunch of sage
small bunch of lovage
1 onion, sliced
2 carrots, sliced
2 celery sticks, sliced
12 black peppercorns

Ask your butcher if the gammon needs soaking, and if so for how long. You can shortcut a lengthy soaking time by putting the gammon joint into a saucepan of cold water, bringing it to the boil, and then discarding the water.

Place the joint in a large saucepan, cover with cold water and bring to the boil, skimming off any scum.

Tie the parsley, sage and lovage together and add them to the pan along with the remaining ingredients. Allow the joint to simmer for 20 minutes per 450g.

When the cooking time has finished, remove the pan from the heat and leave the gammon in the water.

To serve, remove the gammon from the water, take off the rind and thinly slice the meat.

Serve with plain boiled potatoes, spinach, and parsley sauce (see below).

Parsley Sauce

200ml milk
50g butter
50g plain flour
a handful of chopped parsley
salt and white pepper

Heat the milk to just below boiling point.

Melt the butter in a saucepan, stir in the flour and cook for a couple of minutes.

Slowly pour in the hot milk, stirring vigorously, and cook until the sauce thickens. Add the chopped parsley and cook for a further minute or two.

Taste and add salt and white pepper, bearing in mind that the gammon may already be rather salty.

Sausage and Mash

Gone are the days when the only sausages you could readily get were more marmalade than mustard, bready and bland. There is a great number of specialist sausages covering all corners of the culinary globe – Thai chicken, Cajun catfish, coconut and lime lamb are some of the more unlikely combinations we've seen. There's not much better than a good, tactfully seasoned pork sausage.

12 sausages
1kg peeled potatoes – King Edward has a very good flavour and texture – cut into chunks
1 tablespoon salt
75g butter
150ml milk

Preheat the oven to 220°C (425°F), Gas Mark 7.
Put the sausages in one layer in a roasting tin and put them into the oven for about 20 to 30 minutes, until they are nicely brown, shaking the tin from time to time to turn the sausages over.

Meanwhile, put the potatoes into a saucepan with the salt and enough water to cover by about 2 cm. Bring to the boil and cook until tender. Drain in a colander and cover with a clean tea towel to dry them out a bit.

Put the butter and half the milk in the saucepan and return it to the heat. Push the potatoes through a ricer or mouli-legumes into the pan containing the hot milk and butter. Incorporate the mixture with a wooden spoon, adding more milk depending on how firm or otherwise you like your mash.

Onion gravy is the ideal accompaniment. Don't forget the mustard and tomato ketchup either.

Onion Gravy

25g butter
2 onions, finely sliced
splash of red wine vinegar
1 tablespoon sugar
200ml beef stock (see page 246)
salt and pepper

Melt the butter in a shallow pan and gently sweat the onions until they are just beginning to brown. Add the vinegar and allow to bubble almost away. Add the sugar and the stock and simmer, stirring from time to time to reduce to a gravy. Check for seasoning, adding a few grinds of black pepper and some salt if necessary.

Carré d'Agneau

A delicious cut of lamb – far nicer than individual chops; somehow roasting lamb keeps it moist and succulent. It needs very little preparation, especially now that you can buy nicely trimmed racks of lamb in most supermarkets. Discard the frilly paper crowns they sometimes come with unless you're feeling particularly ironic.

2 racks of lamb – 6 to 8 cutlets on each
1 tablespoon olive oil
salt and pepper
150ml red wine
1 tablespoon redcurrant jelly
50ml chicken stock (see page 247) or vegetable (see page 246) or lamb stock

Preheat the oven to 220°C (425°F), Gas Mark 7.

Brush the racks of lamb with some olive oil, sprinkle with salt and pepper and put into the oven for 25 minutes – this will give you rare lamb. If you like it more cooked, cook it for a further 10 to 15 minutes. Remove the lamb from the oven and keep warm.

Skim the fat from the roasting tin, then add the wine, redcurrant jelly and stock to the tin and place over a high heat to reduce, scraping up any bits sticking to the tin. Strain into a warm jug or gravy boat.

Carve the lamb into individual chops and serve them with the gravy and redcurrant jelly.

Gratin dauphinoise (see page 178) is an excellent potato dish to serve with Carré d'Agneau.

Sautéed Kidneys with Mustard

12 lambs' kidneys
45g clarified butter
1 tablespoon Cognac or Armagnac
1 tablespoon Dijon mustard
60ml double cream
splash of red wine vinegar

Split each kidney in half through the core. Using a pair of very sharp scissors, snip away the cores.

Heat the butter in a sauté pan and when it is really hot put in the kidneys, turning them over to brown on all sides. This should take 2 to 3 minutes.

Add the Cognac or Armagnac and carefully light it with a match, standing back until the flames subside. Stir in the mustard, cream and vinegar. Serve immediately on very hot plates.

Fluffy mashed potatoes and a green leafy vegetable are our preferred accompaniments.

Navarin Printanier

Or spring lamb stew. This really captures the flavour of spring – baby vegetables and sweet young lamb. It's an all-in-one dish that improves with sitting in the refrigerator or larder for twenty-four hours, so it is ideal for entertaining.

1 kg lamb shoulder, cut into cubes
8 lamb cutlets
1 bay leaf
a sprig of thyme
1 onion, stuck with 2 cloves
1 carrot, chopped
1 leek, chopped
3 garlic cloves, chopped
200g small carrots
200 small turnips
200g small onions
200g young thin leeks, sliced
100ml white wine
200ml light chicken stock (see page 247)
or lamb stock
200g French beans
200g peas
salt and white pepper
a handful of chopped parsley

Put the meat cubes and the cutlets into a casserole with the bay leaf, thyme, onion stuck with cloves, the chopped carrot, leek, and garlic and add enough water to cover. Bring to a simmer and cook very gently for 1 hour.

Allow the casserole to cool completely and lift off the solidified fat. Remove the pieces of lamb to a clean casserole and strain the liquid over the lamb. Discard the herbs and vegetables.

Add the small carrots, turnips and onions, the sliced leeks, and the white wine and stock and bring to a simmer, allowing it to cook for 15 minutes.

Add the French beans and cook for a further 10 minutes, then add the peas and cook for 5 more minutes. Adjust the seasoning. Allow to cool, then keep in the fridge or larder for up to 24 hours.

Reheat gently to just boiling point, add the parsley and serve on very hot plates.

Roast Leg of Lamb

One of the more glamorous restaurants in the world is the Oustau de Baumanière in Les Baux de Provence where, during the summer, you can sit on a terrace looking down the Rhône valley towards the Camargue and drink delicious Champagne cocktails. Their signature dish, which has been on the menu since it was introduced by the founder of the hotel, Raymond Thuillier, is gigot d'agneau en croûte. It is a dish for two and the leg of lamb is very tender, coming from local milk-fed lambs. Here is a more modest dish using the same delicious cut of lamb.

1 leg of lamb, weighing about 1.5kg to 2kg
4 garlic cloves, finely chopped
50ml olive oil
salt and pepper
a large handful of freshly-cut rosemary sprigs
a handful of thyme
1 teaspoon salt and a few grinds of pepper
100ml white wine
1 tablespoon redcurrant jelly
200ml chicken stock (see page 247)

Preheat the oven to 220°C (425°F), Gas Mark 7.

Have the butcher take out the aitchbone from the leg, and tie up the joint. This gives a neater roast and makes it easy to carve. Weigh the leg.

Mix the garlic with the olive oil – you can do this in a mortar – and smear the mixture over the lamb. Sprinkle with the salt and pepper.

Put the rosemary and thyme in the bottom of a roasting tin and place the lamb on top. Put it into the oven and roast for 15 minutes per 500g, if you like lamb pink, or 20 minutes per 500g if you like it more cooked.

When the lamb is done, transfer it to a carving dish or board and keep warm.

Remove the rosemary and thyme and discard. Spoon any excess fat from the juices in the roasting tin, add the wine and reduce over a high heat, scraping up the bits in the tin. Stir in the redcurrant jelly and the stock and continue to heat until it has reduced a bit further. Adjust the seasoning, if necessary, and strain the gravy into a gravy boat.

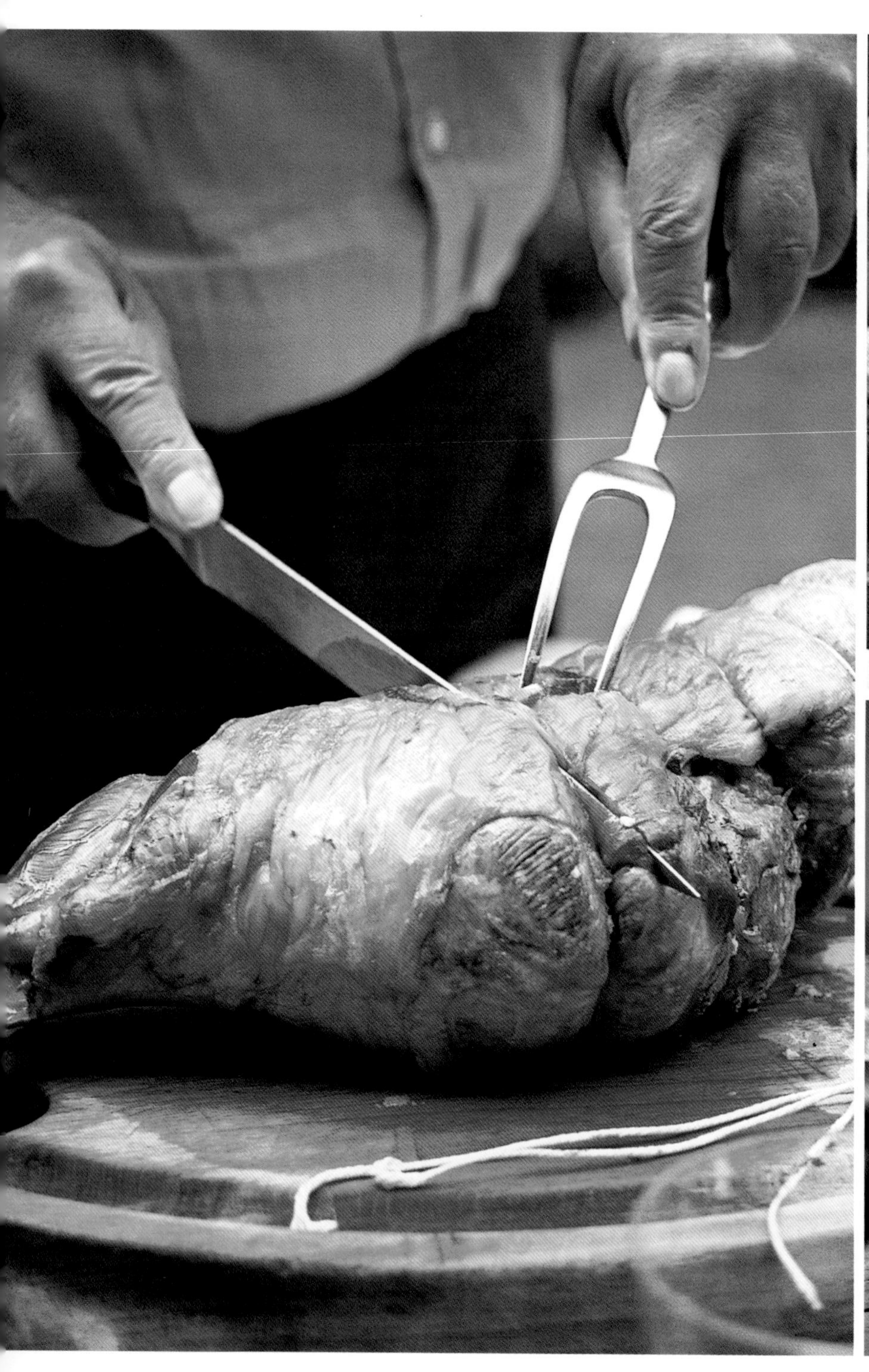

Brochettes of Lamb

A great barbecue dish: tender lamb, charred on the outside and pink within, served with cucumber and yoghurt, green salad, preserved lemon and pitta breads. You can vary the contents of the skewers according to what you want – chicken, mushrooms, firm fish such as monkfish, whatever.

800g lamb leg steaks, cubed
4 garlic cloves, sliced
a sprig of rosemary
a sprig of thyme
20 bay leaves
50ml olive oil
4 red onions, thickly sliced
1 red pepper, thickly sliced
4 lambs kidneys, cored and quartered

Put the lamb, garlic, rosemary and thyme and 4 bay leaves into a large earthenware basin and add the olive oil. Stir everything together, cover and allow to marinate in a cool place for 4 hours or overnight.

Soak 16 bamboo skewers in cold water for 20 minutes.

Remove the lamb from the marinade.

Using 2 skewers for each brochette (this prevents the meat slipping round, making cooking them easier) thread alternate pieces of meat, onion, red pepper and kidney, putting a piece of bay leaf here and there. Don't put too much on each skewer; better to have 8 medium skewers than 4 large ones.

Brush the brochettes generously with the marinade and grill them for about 15 minutes, basting and turning frequently until they are cooked.

Poached Chicken with Tarragon Sauce

a big bunch of tarragon
1 chicken, about 1kg
salt and pepper
1 litre chicken stock (see page 247)
100g butter
100ml double cream
a squeeze of lemon juice

Preheat the oven to 160°C (325°F), Gas Mark 3.

Cut the woody stalks from the tarragon and place them in the bottom of a large lidded casserole or oven-proof saucepan. Cut the tender leaves from the tops of the tarragon and reserve for the sauce. Put the remaining tarragon stalks inside the chicken, together with a few grinds of salt and pepper.

Put the chicken on top of the woody stalks in the casserole or saucepan and pour in the stock. Smear about 25g of the butter on the breast of the chicken and season with salt and pepper. Put on a moderate heat and bring the stock to a simmer. Cover with the lid and put into the oven. Baste every 20 minutes or so and cook for about 1 hour, until the juices run clear when the thigh is pierced with a skewer or fork.

Remove the chicken from the pan and keep it warm. Skim off and discard the fat from the liquid in the casserole and put the casserole over a high heat to boil briskly and to reduce.

Meanwhile, chop the tarragon leaves and put them into a small saucepan with the cream and the remaining butter, heating gently. The sauce should thicken quite a bit on the heat, so slacken it with the boiling stock until you have the consistency of thin cream. Add salt and pepper and a squeeze of lemon to taste, and keep hot.

Carve the chicken and serve the tarragon sauce separately.

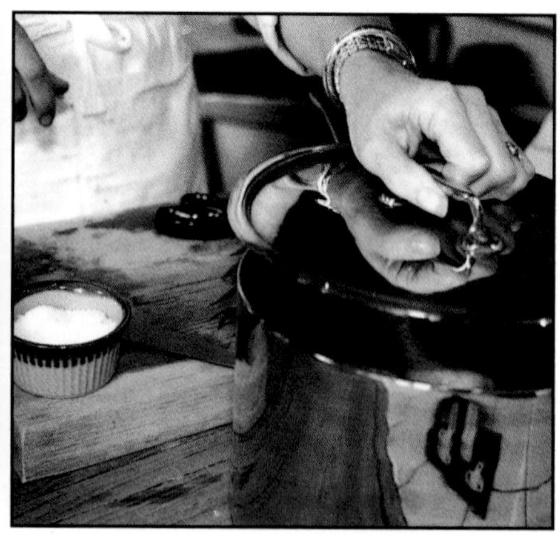

Roast Chicken

One of the enduringly popular meals – a simple roast chicken, roast potatoes, peas and gravy. Whenever we have been abroad for any length of time it's the thing we most look forward to upon our return – roast chicken and a nice big bath. At last people tend to be turning away from those battery-reared chickens that, while invariably cheap, are fairly tasteless at best and really nasty-tasting otherwise. You can now buy really good chickens in supermarkets, farmers' markets and butchers. Certainly you may have to pay more for a carefully-reared chicken but the resulting dish is far superior and, in our opinion, worth it. A roast chicken is a marvellous thing, generally providing more than just one meal. There are always leftovers sufficient for at least one sandwich, and the remaining carcass provides the stock for a nourishing soup.

1 roasting chicken, about 1.5kg
salt and pepper
30g butter
150g of thin slices of streaky bacon rashers (optional)
30ml white wine
150ml chicken stock (see page 247)

Preheat the oven to 200°C (400°F), Gas Mark 6.

Sprinkle the inside of the chicken with salt and pepper and smear the butter on the breasts. You can then add a covering of thin slices of streaky bacon. Place the bird in a roasting tin and cover lightly with foil.

Roast in the oven for 20 minutes per 500g, basting frequently. Remove the foil and bacon from the chicken for the final 15 minutes to gild the breast. The chicken is cooked when the juices run clear when the thighs are skewered.

Transfer the bird to a platter and keep warm. It is easier to carve and more tender if it rests for 10 to 15 minutes after it has finished roasting.

Pour the wine and stock into the roasting tin and bring to the boil, stirring with a spoon to dislodge the sediment. Then strain into a gravy boat and serve with the carved chicken.

Coq au Vin

2 tablespoons duck fat or clarified butter
1 chicken, about 1.5kg, jointed into 4 portions
200g smoked bacon, diced
2 garlic cloves, sliced
750ml red wine
1 tablespoon redcurrant jelly
250g shallots or small onions
250g button mushrooms
4 slices of bread, cut into triangles
a large handful of chopped parsley
salt and pepper

Preheat the oven to 160°C (325°F), Gas Mark 3.

Heat half the fat or butter in a sauté pan, sauté the chicken until golden and then place in a lidded casserole.

Brown the bacon pieces in the sauté pan, adding the sliced garlic for the last 30 seconds. Add the bacon and garlic to the chicken.

Pour off the fat from the pan, add the wine and redcurrant jelly and bring to the boil, scraping up the bits in the pan. Then pour over the chicken and bacon.

Sauté the onions or shallots in the remaining fat or butter, and when they are burnished add them to the casserole. Do the same with the mushrooms. Cover the casserole and put into the oven for 45 minutes.

A few minutes before the chicken is ready, reheat the fat left in the pan and fry the slices of bread until golden. Press the chopped parsley on to one side.

When the bird is cooked, skim off any remaining fat. Check the seasoning of the casserole, and serve the chicken on very hot plates, with the triangles of fried parsleyed bread.

Serve boiled potatoes to accompany, with a good robust red from Beaune.

Roast Goose

Although becoming more popular and therefore readily available, you will still need to order a goose from your butcher. We always look for a nice fatty one – the dripping gives us a few months of really wonderful roast vegetables. When you get it home, unwrap the goose, poke it all over with a fine larding needle and leave it exposed in a cool place or the refrigerator.

1 goose
salt and pepper
4 onions
a handful of sage leaves
the goose liver

Preheat the oven to 200°C (400°F), Gas Mark 6.

Sprinkle the inside of the goose with salt and pepper, then roughly chop two of the onions and stuff them, with the sage leaves, into the cavity. Rub salt all over the skin of the goose and weigh it. Put a large roasting tin on the floor of your oven and adjust the racks so that the goose can sit comfortably directly on a rack.

Put the goose on the rack in the oven and roast for 30 minutes per 500g. Don't baste it, but remember to empty the roasting tin of drippings into a large bowl from time to time.

When the goose is cooked, put it on a carving dish or board and allow it to rest for about 30 minutes.

At the last minute, briefly sauté the liver and either quietly eat it yourself, or divide it up among your diners.

Carve thin slices from the goose, including some skin with each slice, and serve with apple sauce and goose gravy (see opposite).

Serve with roast potatoes (see page 168); braised red cabbage (see page 173) is rather good with this too.

Goose Gravy

- the goose giblets – reserve the liver for sautéing (see opposite)
- 2 onions, coarsely chopped
- 2 carrots, coarsely chopped
- 2 sticks of celery, coarsely chopped
- 2 leeks, coarsely chopped
- 100ml port or Madeira
- 300ml chicken stock (see page 247)
- 1 tablespoon apple jelly
- salt and pepper

Preheat the oven to 200°C (400°F), Gas Mark 6.

Put the goose giblets, onions, carrots, celery and leeks into a small roasting tin and put into the oven for 30 minutes. Remove the tin from the oven.

On top of the stove, pour the port or Madeira into the roasting tin and on a moderate heat scrape up any bits clinging to the bottom. Transfer the contents of the tin to a saucepan and add the chicken stock and apple jelly. Bring to a simmer and allow to blip away for 30 to 45 minutes.

Pour the gravy through a conical strainer into a clean pan and remove as much fat as possible. Season with salt and pepper, return to the boil, then serve.

Apple Sauce

- 2 large or 3 medium cooking apples, peeled, cored and chopped – Bramleys have the best texture
- 2 tablespoons sugar
- a squeeze of lemon juice

Put the apples together with the sugar and lemon juice into a small stainless or enamelled pan. Add 2 tablespoons water and cook very gently until the apples have exploded and collapsed.

Break up the apples with a wooden spoon, or if you like an apple purée, push them through a sieve or mouli-legumes.

Serve the sauce at room temperature.

You can add a couple of cloves or a pinch of cinnamon for a spicier version.

Grilled Spatchcock Poussin

Succulent and tender, small poussin chickens are ideal for grilling. Get your butcher to split (spatchcock) them, or do it yourself by cutting down the back and pressing the birds flat (poultry shears are invaluable for this job, though stout scissors will probably do). You can use wooden or steel skewers to help keep them flat. These chickens are lovely cooked over a wood-fired grill.

4 poussin chickens, spatchcocked
juice of two lemons
2 tbsp olive oil, plus extra for grilling
a sprig of thyme, finely chopped
a sprig of marjoram, finely chopped
salt and pepper

Sprinkle both sides of the chickens with the lemon juice, olive oil and finely chopped herbs. Then set them aside to marinate at room-temperature for about an hour.

Heat the grill to its hottest setting, or, if using a wood-fired grill, make sure that your wood has burned down to white-hot embers. Place the chickens on a grilling rack, brush with some olive oil and sprinkle on some salt and pepper. Grill, skin side first, for 5 to 6 minutes. Turn the chickens over, brush with more oil, sprinkle with some more salt and pepper and grill for a further 5 to 6 minutes.

To test whether the birds are done, push a skewer or the tip of a sharp knife into the thickest part of the thigh. The juices will run clear when the bird is cooked.

Serve each chicken with lemon wedges and a green salad.

Shortcrust Pastry

The trick to making successful shortcrust pastry, is to ensure that everything is cold, including your hands. This recipe makes about 500g of pastry.

350g plain flour
1 teaspoon salt
150g butter or lard, or a 50/50 mixture, diced
2 egg yolks, beaten
iced water (optional)

Sift the flour and salt into a roomy bowl. Really lightly rub the fat into the flour – coarse breadcrumbs is the texture you are aiming for. Add the egg yolks and, with a palette knife, bring the dough together – you may need to sprinkle on a dash of iced water, but don't get the dough too wet. Make a ball, wrap in clingfilm and refrigerate for 20 minutes before using.

Chicken and Leek Pie

A basic savoury pie that can be filled with all sorts of other ingredients – game, rabbit, vegetables; the important thing to remember, though, is not too many different ingredients in one pie or it will become a bit of a dog's dinner. We make the pies in small individual enamelled pie dishes, you know, the white ones with a dark blue rim, but one large pie looks very good too.

- 800g chicken breast or thigh meat, in large pieces
- 1 onion, chopped
- 1 leek, chopped
- 1 carrot, chopped
- 1 stick of celery, chopped
- 50g butter
- 600g leeks, white parts only, finely sliced
- 2 onions, finely sliced
- 50g plain flour
- 200ml milk, heated
- 150ml double cream, heated
- a handful of finely chopped parsley
- salt and white pepper
- 500g pastry – shortcrust (see opposite) or puff
- 1 egg yolk mixed with 1 tablespoon milk to make an egg wash

Put the chicken into a casserole with the chopped onion, leek, carrot and celery. Barely cover with water and bring to a simmer. Gently poach the chicken for 20 minutes and then allow to cool.

Preheat the oven to 190°C (375°F), Gas Mark 5.

Remove the chicken from the casserole and cut into bite-sized pieces. Discard the vegetables but reserve the chicken stock.

Melt the butter in a large saucepan and sweat the sliced leeks and onions until softened. Stir in the flour and cook for about 2 minutes. Stir in the milk and cream and cook gently while still stirring until thickened to a sauce. Fold in the chicken pieces and the chopped parsley. If the sauce is now too thick, slacken it with a little of the reserved stock. Add salt and pepper to taste and allow to cool.

Roll out the pastry to about 5mm thick and use about two-thirds to line a 1 litre pie dish or four individual dishes. Spoon in the chicken filling and dampen the edges of the pastry base.

Roll out the remaining pastry to make a lid(s) and cover the pie(s). Press the pastry edges together and trim with a sharp knife. Brush the surface of the pie(s) with the egg wash and cut a small slash in the top of the pie(s) to allow the steam to escape. Bake for 35 minutes if you are cooking individual pies, or 1 hour for a single large pie.

Roast and Braised Game Birds

The moors, fields, waters and skies abound with feathered game, more so since shooting has become a hugely popular and sought-after sport. Organised driven shoots have become a major rural industry and a 'gun' at a good shoot is something to guard jealously. This has resulted in the routine 'seeding' of suitable tracts of land with young pheasant or partridge chicks before the beginning of the season, feeding them large quantities of game pellets then releasing the fat and rather indolent birds to the mercies of sometimes rather inept shooters. There have been stories of truly offensive numbers of birds bagged in a day's shooting, so many that those unclaimed have been ploughed into the land. However, you can avoid all this by making friends with your local butcher and encouraging him to procure the unquestionably delicious results of the barbaric sport on your behalf.

The game season is relatively short – autumn and winter – and the best time for roasting the birds is when they are young. Older birds, while in no way inferior in flavour, benefit more fully from gentle braising.

Considered rather odd by our game-mad European neighbours, we like our game, well, gamey. This is achieved by hanging the birds for anything between four and twelve days, depending on the size and species, giving the flesh time to develop its distinctive flavour.

When buying young pheasants or partridges, choose nice fat, firm birds, looking for flexible breastbones and soft, rounded spurs. Young partridges have paler leg colourings than their older brethren, while pigeon legs turn from pink to red with age.

Roasting birds is possibly the simplest way of cooking them. The important thing is that the birds should be young and well-protected with a layer of fat. The cooking time is short: pheasants take about 25 minutes in a hot oven, partridges about 15, smaller birds even less.

The best of all feathered game is grouse, and roast grouse is one of the great dishes of the world. Frequently asked what our most desirable meal would consist of, the answer is always the same: langoustines, roast grouse, Scottish raspberries – nicely plain if not a little luxurious.

Roast Grouse

Perhaps it's because the season is so short and they are so eagerly anticipated that we think there really is nothing better than roast grouse, and the accompanying bread sauce and game chips. In counting off the days from the Glorious Twelfth to when the birds have been properly hung and we can eat the first grouse of the season, we are rather like children opening the windows of our Advent calendar, counting the days until Christmas. If the livers are unavailable you can substitute chicken or duck livers, or foie gras, or just serve the birds on the fried bread.

knob of butter
4 grouse, including their livers if possible
4 rashers of streaky bacon, or slices of pork back fat
2 tablespoons clarified butter
4 slices of bread, crusts removed
20ml red wine
40ml good chicken stock (see page 247)
salt and pepper
a large bunch of watercress

Preheat the oven to 200°C (400°F), Gas Mark 6.

Put a smear of butter on the breasts of each bird then cut the bacon or fat slices in half and cover the breasts, tying them with fine string. Place in a roasting tin and put into the oven for 14 minutes.

Meanwhile, heat the clarified butter in a sauté pan and fry the livers briefly to seal; they should be pink within. Remove the livers from the pan and set aside.

In the same pan fry the bread until it is golden on both sides. Mash the livers and spread on the fried bread, then keep the slices warm.

When the grouse are ready, take the roasting tin from the oven, untie the bacon or pork fat and take it off. Return the birds to the oven for a further 3 minutes, to gild the breasts.

Place the fried bread on a hot serving platter, then put a grouse on each slice and put the platter in a warm place to rest.

Put the roasting tin on the hob and stir in the wine to dislodge the sediment. Then add the chicken stock, and salt and pepper to taste, and simmer to reduce to a light gravy.

Serve the grouse, accompanied by a bunch of watercress, on very hot plates, with the gravy and bread sauce (see opposite). Game chips are the traditional potato dish to serve with grouse.

Bread Sauce

Bread sauce is the essential accompaniment to roast grouse. Use decent white bread – the bagged, sliced, sandwich loaf delivers a rather nasty, greyish, slimy sauce that one could really do without.

1 small onion, chopped
1 bay leaf
3 cloves
a couple of blades of mace, or a pinch of grated nutmeg
300ml full fat milk
150g day-old bread, crusts off, and whizzed into fine breadcrumbs
a knob of butter or a tablespoon of double cream – or both
salt

Put the onion, bay leaf, cloves and mace or nutmeg into a pan with the milk and bring to the boil. Remove the pan from the heat and allow to sit for a couple of hours, letting the flavours merge into the milk.

About 30 minutes before you want to serve the sauce, strain the milk into a clean pan and add the breadcrumbs. Simmer for 20 minutes, stirring occasionally. Add the butter and/or cream and salt to taste.

If you need to keep the sauce for a while, film the surface with some milk and then stir it in just before serving.

Pigeon and Peas

A classic of the cuisine de terroir *repertoire. You can buy farmed pigeons fairly readily; they are plumper and more tender than their wild cousins.*

30g butter
4 shallots, finely chopped
75g smoked streaky bacon or pancetta, chopped
2 plump wild pigeons, or 4 farmed pigeons
500ml light chicken stock (see page 247)
750g shelled or frozen petits pois
a bunch of parsley, chopped

Melt the butter in a large flameproof casserole and gently sauté the shallots and bacon or pancetta. Add the pigeons to the casserole and brown gently, stirring frequently, for about 20 minutes.

Add the stock, bring to a simmer, and then add the peas. Cover the casserole and cook very gently for 30 minutes.

Remove the pigeons to a warm platter and keep warm.

Raise the heat under the casserole, add the parsley and cook for 15 minutes more. Spoon the peas and reduced juices over the pigeons and serve immediately on very hot plates.

Salmis of Pheasant

Salmis is a derivation from the rather more elaborate salmigondis, *in turn a variation of salmagundy, the legendary dish of miscellaneous cold cuts laid out in concentric circles. You can make this dish with other feathered game birds, indeed any combination of birds works very well. A salmis is a marvellous way to cook the older, tired birds that are bagged towards the end of the season.*

1 pheasant
70g butter
1 onion, finely chopped
1 carrot, finely chopped
1 stick of celery, finely chopped
50ml Cognac
200ml red wine
400ml good game stock
salt and pepper
150g button mushrooms
1 tablespoon butter
a squeeze of lemon juice

Preheat the oven to 190°C (375°F), Gas Mark 5.

Place the bird in a roasting tin and roast in the oven for 15 minutes.

Meanwhile, melt the butter in a flameproof casserole and cook the onion, carrot and celery over a low heat.

Take the birds from the oven and, when cool enough, carve into leg and breast portions, placing them in an ovenproof dish to catch any juices. Return the skin and carcasses to the casserole.

Warm the Cognac in a small saucepan, set it alight and pour it carefully into the casserole. When the flames have died down, add the red wine, stock, and some salt and pepper to taste. Bring to a simmer and cook gently for 30 minutes.

Preheat the oven to 180°C (350°F), Gas Mark 4.

Meanwhile, cook the mushrooms very gently in the butter and lemon juice, then add them to the pheasant portions.

Strain the juices in the casserole over the pheasant in the ovenproof dish. Place the dish in the oven for 15 minutes to finish cooking.

Serve the salmis with triangles of fried bread and a braised vegetable such as red cabbage or chicory.

Civet of Hare

Rich and delicious, hare is a special treat for a dull winter day. There is, in the classic repertoire, a dish of unparalleled richness and magnificence – lièvre à la royale – a hare stuffed with foie gras, braised in at least two bottles of burgundy and embellished with a Cognac sauce. We memorably ate it as guests of Moët et Chandon at the delightful Château de Saran, (Moët et Chandon's chateau in the Champagne region of France), in sparkling company and drinking exceptional vintage champagne. Here is a more modest though equally delicious recipe.

1 hare
200ml olive oil
30g butter
200g smoked bacon, cut into cubes
1 fat garlic clove, crushed
20 button onions
250g button mushrooms
2 tablespoons redcurrant jelly
salt and pepper

For the marinade:
3 large onions, sliced
1 carrot, sliced
500ml red wine
1 tablespoon Cognac or Armagnac
50ml oil
a bay leaf
a sprig of thyme
pepper

Have your butcher cut up the hare, or do it yourself, into thighs, forelegs, and the saddle in 4 pieces, reserving the liver and blood. Put the meat into a dish with the marinade ingredients. Cover and leave to marinate in a cool place for 24 hours.

The following day, remove and dry the pieces of hare, reserving the vegetables and the marinade.

Heat the oil and butter in a sauté pan and brown the pieces of hare on each side, transferring the cooked pieces to a flameproof casserole. Put the sliced onions and carrot from the marinade, and the bacon and garlic, into the pan and allow them to brown before adding them to the casserole. Pour in enough of the marinade liquid to cover the hare, together with the bay leaf and sprig of thyme. Bring to a simmer, cover and cook gently for 2 hours.

Meanwhile, sauté the onions and mushrooms in the sauté pan.

When the hare is cooked, remove the pieces to a platter, adding the mushrooms and onions.

Chop up the liver and mix with the reserved blood, adding it to the cooking juices, together with the redcurrant jelly, and salt and pepper to taste. Bring to a simmer then strain over the hare.

Serve the civet very hot, with fried bread and plain boiled potatoes.

Wood-grilled Rabbit

You can now get really good farmed rabbits that are tender and tasty and ideal for barbecues. Marinating the rabbit for a day before cooking adds flavour, but it's not really necessary if you want instant gratification.

- 1 rabbit, jointed into legs, saddle and forelegs
- 4 garlic cloves, thickly sliced
- a bunch of herbs – rosemary, thyme, parsley and sage – coarsely chopped
- 2 tablespoons olive oil

Place the rabbit pieces in a large bowl and strew with the garlic and herbs. Add the olive oil and put in the fridge for 24 hours, turning the pieces over a couple of times.

Light your fire in the usual way and allow the wood to burn down to really hot embers with no flames.

Take the rabbit from the bowl, shaking off any loose bits of twig, and place on the fire for 15 to 20 minutes until cooked through and charred round the edges. When pierced with a skewer, the juices should run clear.

A large green salad with a garlicky dressing and some crusty bread, washed down with a merlot from the Pays d'Oc, make this a meal to enjoy al fresco.

If you don't have a wood-fired grill, or a barbeque, you can use an electric or gas grill. Let it get really hot before you begin cooking.

Ragu Sauce

Spag rag, also known as spag bol, is the mainstay of student entertaining: what could be simpler – mince, a can of tomatoes and a packet of spaghetti? Well, this isn't quite that simple, but is infinitely more delicious. We generally use lamb or veal, finding it gives a rounder flavour and texture, but it works with minced beef. It is an extremely useful sauce – you can use it for lasagne, cannelloni or any other pasta dish. The secret lies in cooking the sauce for hours and hours to achieve homogenised unctuousness.

100ml olive oil
50g butter
50g smoked bacon, preferably pancetta, cubed
1 onion, finely chopped
2 garlic cloves, finely chopped
1 carrot, finely chopped
1 stick of celery, finely chopped
500g minced lamb, veal or beef
250ml red wine
500g tomatoes – canned, passata or really ripe plum tomatoes, skinned and seeded
a sprig of thyme
a bay leaf
salt and pepper

Preheat the oven to 150°C (300°F), Gas Mark 2.

Heat the oil and butter in a large flameproof casserole, put in the bacon, onion, garlic, carrot and celery and cook gently until the vegetables have softened. Add the minced meat and, stirring, allow it to turn from pink to beige. Pour in the red wine and let it bubble almost away, stirring all the while. Tip in the tomatoes, thyme and bay leaf, add salt and pepper to taste, and bring to a gentle simmer.

Cover, and then either cook the ragu on top of the stove with a heat diffuser, or place it in the oven for 3 hours, checking from time to time that the sauce is not too dry – if it is stir in 1 tablespoon of water and turn the heat down a notch. The finished sauce should be thick and dark with no discernible elements identifiable within.

Spaghetti alle Vongole

This is the white version of clam sauce. You can make it tomatoey with the addition of a couple of skinned, deseeded and chopped tomatoes.

4kg small clams
75ml olive oil
2 garlic cloves, chopped
100ml white wine
1 chilli, finely minced (optional)
a handful of parsley, finely chopped
400g spaghetti or the finer spaghettini (200g if you are having this as a starter)
salt and pepper

Wash the clams and leave them to soak in cold water for 30 minutes, changing it a few times.

Heat the olive oil in a large saucepan and sauté the garlic gently. Turn up the heat, pour in the wine and clams, and chilli, if using, and cook, covered for 5 to 8 minutes until the clam shells open, shaking the pan from time to time.

When the clam shells have opened, add the parsley.

Meanwhile, cook the pasta according to the packet instructions, then drain it thoroughly and mix it into the clams.

Season with salt and pepper and serve immediately on hot plates.

If you can't get fresh clams, Italian bottled clams are a very suitable and quick substitute. Use 250g, halve the amount of wine and heat the clams gently, without allowing them to boil.

Lasagne al Forno

It's now quite easy to get fresh lasagne in the chilled cabinets of most supermarkets. Dried lasagne, too, has become easier to use – you no longer have to pre-cook most brands. Use the ragu sauce recipe (see p156), lashings of béchamel sauce, nutmeg and Parmesan cheese.

250g ragu sauce (see page 156)
300g lasagne sheets
a scrape of nutmeg
50g Parmesan cheese, shaved

For the béchamel sauce:
300ml milk
1 small onion, chopped
1 bay leaf
2 blades of mace
30g butter
30g flour
salt and white pepper

Preheat the oven to 200°C (400°F), Gas Mark 6.

Begin to prepare the béchamel sauce, by heating the milk to boiling point with the onion, bay leaf and mace. Remove from the heat, cover and allow to stand.

Liberally butter a 1.5 to 2-litre baking dish and spread a couple of spoonfuls of ragu sauce over the bottom. Lay sheets of lasagne in a single layer over the sauce, add another layer of ragu, then more lasagne and repeat until ragu and lasagne have been used up. We usually make 3 or 4 complete layers.

To finish the béchamel sauce, melt the butter in a large saucepan, stir in the flour and cook gently for a couple of minutes. Strain the hot, flavoured milk through a conical sieve into the saucepan, stirring all the time. Cook, still stirring, until the sauce thickens. Taste and add salt and white pepper as necessary, remembering that the ragu sauce will probably be quite savoury.

Pour the béchamel sauce over the lasagne, then grate some nutmeg on top and scatter with Parmesan shavings.

Bake the lasagne for 30 to 40 minutes until it is golden and bubbling.

Serve with a crisp green salad.

Spaghetti Carbonara

Here's a quick pasta dish that you can easily make if friends turn up unexpectedly – a sort of Italian bacon and eggs.

400g smoked bacon or pancetta, cut into lardons
4 egg yolks
100ml double cream
500g spaghetti
salt and pepper
grated Parmesan cheese, to serve

Sauté the bacon or pancetta gently until just turning golden.

Beat the egg yolks and cream together in a bowl.

Cook the pasta in a large quantity of salted boiling water, following the directions on the pack, until al dente.

Drain the pasta, return it to the pan and quickly stir the egg and cream mixture – it will thicken in the heat of the pasta – then stir in the bacon or pancetta. Season with salt and pepper.

Serve immediately on large heated plates with plenty of grated Parmesan.

Tomato Sauce for Pasta

A really plain and simple sauce. Use ripe juicy tomatoes with lots of flavour.

2 tablespoons olive oil
a bunch of spring onions, sliced
2 garlic cloves, chopped
500g tomatoes, skinned, deseeded and coarsely chopped
salt and pepper
a pinch of sugar
a squeeze of lemon juice
olive oil, to serve
shredded basil leaves, to serve

Gently heat the oil in a pan and sweat the onions and garlic until transparent. Add the tomatoes and allow to cook very gently – they will melt into a purée.

Taste and add salt, pepper and perhaps some sugar if you think it necessary. Cook until the sauce has thickened to the consistency you like. Add a squeeze of lemon juice to perk up the sauce.

Serve the sauce spooned over freshly cooked pasta. Drizzle with olive oil, and scatter with some shredded basil leaves.

Risotto Primavera

This is a real taste of spring. Use very young vegetables and light chicken stock and the resulting risotto is not only delicious but also extremely pretty – white rice with lovely green vegetables.

200g each of peas, French beans, broad beans, courgettes, artichokes or asparagus – 800g vegetables in all
750ml chicken stock (see page 247)
100g butter
20ml olive oil
4 spring onions, sliced
200g risotto rice – Arborio or carnaroli
a small bunch of herbs – parsley, mint, tarragon, very finely chopped
100g Parmesan cheese, finely grated, plus extra to serve

Prepare the vegetables: pod the peas; top and tail the French beans, and cut them into 2cm lengths. Shell the broad beans; slice the courgettes; discard the tough leaves from the artichokes and finely slice the remainder. Remove and discard the tough parts of the stalks of the asparagus, then chop the rest into 2cm lengths. Blanch each vegetable separately in lightly salted boiling water.

Pour the stock into a saucepan and heat it to boiling point. Meanwhile, heat 25g of the butter with the olive oil in a large sauté pan, add the spring onions and cook them slowly without browning. Add the risotto rice and cook it gently for about 2 minutes in the butter and oil until it is well coated.

Add two ladlefuls of boiling stock and stir, allowing it to be absorbed. Gradually add more stock as needed, stirring from time to time, allowing the rice to bubble and absorb the stock. Add the vegetables and herbs with the last amount of stock; fold in the remaining butter and the Parmesan cheese.

Serve on hot plates, scattered with some more grated Parmesan.

Risotto with Chicken Livers

People tend to think that risotto is a lot of hard work, that there is going to be hours of stirring a hot, steamy pot and that the rice will never cook properly. In fact, a risotto is relatively simple to make, the important ingredient being the rice – it really has to be one of the round, short-grain Italian varieties – usually labelled arborio, carnaroli or vialone nano. American long-grain rice won't really do for risotto, though it is ideal for pilaffs.

1 litre chicken stock (see page 247) or vegetable stock (see page 246)
100g butter
20ml olive oil
2 shallots, finely chopped
220g arborio, carnaroli or vialone nano rice
500g chicken livers, cleaned
a sprig of thyme, leaves finely chopped
100g Parmesan cheese, finely grated

Put the stock to heat in a saucepan. Meanwhile, heat 25g of the butter with the olive oil in a large sauté pan, add the shallots and cook them slowly until they are transluscent. Add the rice and cook it gently in the butter and oil for about 2 minutes until it is well coated.

Add 2 ladlefuls of simmering stock and stir it in, allowing it to bubble. Keep adding the stock a ladleful at a time, allowing it to be absorbed as it bubbles.

Meanwhile, melt another 25g of butter in a frying pan and when it sizzles, tip in the chicken livers and the thyme leaves, shaking the pan to keep the livers moving about. Cook them until they are nicely browned on the outside, but still rosy inside, by which time the rice should be tender. Add the remaining butter and half the Parmesan to the rice and stir it in.

Serve the risotto in large soup plates with the chicken livers on top, and with the rest of the Parmesan.

Kedgeree

We like this as a scratch dish, that is to say not made from left-over fish or rice. Traditionally served for breakfast, it makes a very good light lunch or supper.

500g smoked haddock
splash of sunflower oil
1 large onion, finely chopped
200g basmati rice
1 teaspoon curry powder or paste
2 tablespoons double cream
40g butter
small handful of finely chopped parsley
4 eggs, hard-boiled, shelled and kept in a basin of very hot water
mango chutney, to serve

Cook the smoked haddock in barely simmering water for about 5 minutes. Lift the fish from the liquid (reserve this), remove the bones and skin and then flake the fish.

Heat the oil in a large sauté pan, add the onion and fry gently until it is transparent and just becoming golden. Stir in the rice and about 500ml of the water in which the fish was cooked, and the curry powder or paste. Bring the whole lot to the boil, cover the pan and simmer for 10 to 12 minutes, or according to the instructions on the packet, until the rice is just tender.

Stir the double cream and the butter into the cooked rice, then gently fold in the flaked fish and the chopped parsley. Quarter the eggs.

Serve the kedgeree on very hot plates, topped with the egg quarters. Mango chutney is the perfect accompaniment.

Roast Potatoes

Ever popular, roast potatoes can sometimes not live up to expectations – they may be soggy, greasy, hard and not at all nice. There are a few things you can do to make sure that your potatoes nearly always satisfy the most picky potato fancier. One of the important things to remember is that you should wait for the potatoes, and not have them waiting for you. They will take about 1 hour, so time the start of the cooking to coincide with when you want to eat them.

800g King Edward or Maris Piper potatoes
1 tablespoon salt
2 tablespoons dripping – beef, goose or chicken

Preheat the oven to 220°C (400°F), Gas Mark 6.

Cut the potatoes in half, or if they are large, quarters. Put them with the salt and enough water to cover in a pan, bring to the boil and cook for 12 minutes.

Drain the potatoes well, put them back in the pan and cover them with a clean, folded tea towel and the lid.

Meanwhile, put the dripping into a roasting tin large enough to accommodate the potatoes in one layer. Put the tin in the oven and allow the dripping to get really hot – just about smoking.

Shake the pan of potatoes gently then, when they are really dry, carefully tip them into the roasting tin of hot dripping. Move the potatoes around with a wooden spatula to coat them evenly with the dripping and put them in the oven for about 1 hour. Give them a turn every 20 minutes or so to make sure that they brown evenly.

Pommes Frites

Chips border on the things to save for when eating in restaurants – we rarely cook them and if we do we only cook for two people. We don't have a deep-fat fryer and we can't stand the smell of hot sunflower, grapeseed or corn oil, preferring to deep-fry in beef dripping. So when we do cook chips we tend to make the Jenga variety rather than thin straw fries. The best we've ever eaten were Heston Blumenthal's at the Fat Duck in Bray – hopefully he still makes them.

Serves 2

2 large baking potatoes – King Edward behaves magnificently
1 kg beef dripping
salt

Scrub the potatoes and leave the skins on, or peel them as you wish. Cut each potato lengthways into large chips, about 2cm square; you will only get about six chips from each potato, but that's enough for one person.

Rinse the chips well in cold water then dry them in kitchen paper or a clean tea towel. They must be really dry.

Heat the dripping in a roomy saucepan until it is hot enough to fry a cube of bread to golden crisp almost immediately.

Put the potatoes into a frying basket and carefully lower it into the hot oil. The potatoes will seethe most satisfactorily. Gently shake the basket from time to time to prevent the chips sticking together.

When the chips are a very pale lemon colour, lift the basket out of the pan, allowing the dripping to drip back into it. After about 1 minute lower the chips back into the hot dripping and fry until they become golden and crisp.

Sprinkle the chips with salt and serve them immediately.

When the dripping has cooled you can pour it through a double layer of muslin into a container and keep it in the fridge for about 2 months, reusing it whenever you need to.

Sautéed Potatoes

These potatoes go well with almost everything – steak, fish, chicken and particularly bacon and eggs.

800g firm, waxy potatoes – Charlotte, Pink Fir Apple and La Ratte are good
2 tablespoons clarified butter, olive oil or goose dripping
a few sage leaves, finely shredded (optional)
salt

Put the potatoes into a pan of cold water, adding 1 tablespoon salt. Bring to the boil and simmer for 15 minutes. Drain, and when cool enough to handle, peel them and slice into rounds or ovals.

Heat the butter or oil in a large sauté pan and add the potatoes, keeping them in one layer. You may have to do them in batches, depending on the size of your pan. Turn the slices over from time to time and cook until they are golden brown.

Just before they are ready, add the sage leaves if you are using them. Sprinkle with salt and serve immediately.

Champ

1 kg potatoes – King Edward or similar – quartered
250ml milk
100g butter
a bunch of spring onions, sliced
salt and white pepper

Put the potatoes in a pan of salted water and boil until tender. Drain, return the potatoes to the pan and cover with a folded tea towel.

Bring the milk and butter to a boil and add the spring onions, allowing them to simmer for about 5 minutes.

Push the potatoes through a ricer or a mouli-legumes, or mash them with a masher, add the milk/cream/onion and mix well. Season with salt and pepper and serve very hot.

Braised Endives

Or chicory. The pale lemon-tipped, tightly-furled buds, with their slightly bitter crispness, work well as a salad, and are particularly good braised, when the bitterness is transformed into a sort of caramel sweetness. The best endives are available during the winter. Braised endives are an excellent accompaniment to grilled meat or fish.

4 endives (chicory)
2 tablespoons butter
50ml chicken stock (see page 247)

Remove any dark or damaged leaves and cut the endives in half lengthways. If the core is large, trim it out.

Melt the butter in a large sauté pan over a moderate heat and put in the endives, cut side down. Shake the pan from time to time to prevent the endives sticking. When they have browned a bit round the edges, turn them over and brown the other side.

Turn the endives back on to their cut side and add the stock, turn the heat down to a bare simmer and allow them to cook for about 20 minutes until completely tender. Watch that the liquid doesn't dry out too much during the cooking.

When the endives are cooked, turn up the heat to reduce any residual liquid to a sticky syrup.

You can cook fennel in much the same way, cutting the bulbs into quarters and cooking them for about 30 minutes.

Braised Lettuces with Peas

4 Little Gem lettuces
50g butter
pinch of sugar
pinch of salt
300g peas – shelled weight
50ml light vegetable stock (see page 246)
6 to 8 mint leaves, shredded

Discard the outer lettuce leaves, then halve them lengthways and trim the cores.

Melt the butter in a shallow sauté pan and very gently soften the lettuces in the hot butter.

Sprinkle the sugar and salt on the lettuces, add the peas and the stock and simmer gently for about 15 minutes. Add the mint leaves during the last 5 minutes.

Serve hot as a vegetable accompaniment, or at room temperature as a salad.

Braised Red Cabbage

This delicious winter vegetable keeps well and is very good with roasts, game dishes and sausages.

20g butter
1 onion, finely sliced
2 apples, peeled, cored and sliced
1 red cabbage, finely sliced
3 tablespoons light brown sugar
3 tablespoons red wine vinegar
50ml light chicken stock (see page 247)
 or vegetable stock (see page 246)
a bunch of thyme
salt and pepper
a squeeze of lemon

Preheat the oven to 160°C (325°F), Gas Mark 3.

Melt the butter in a large flameproof casserole, add the onion and apples and cook gently until they have wilted. Add the cabbage, sugar, vinegar, stock and thyme. Bring to a simmer, cover with a tight-fitting lid and cook very gently in the oven (or on top of the stove) for about 1½ hours until tender.

When the cabbage is cooked, taste for seasoning and if you think it needs perking up, add a squeeze of lemon juice.

You can vary the flavouring, replacing the thyme with a few cloves and a pinch of cinnamon, or even a couple of crushed juniper berries.

Roast Root Vegetables

Most root vegetables roast very satisfactorily if you cut them into pieces much the same size as you would for roast potatoes. The heat of the oven and absence of water really intensify their flavours.

800g root vegetables – parsnips, celeriac, Jerusalem artichokes, beetroots, carrots – chopped
salt
2 tablespoons dripping – goose is wonderful – or chicken or olive oil

Preheat the oven to 220°C (425°F), Gas Mark 7.

Blanch the vegetables separately in salted boiling water for 10 minutes each.

Meanwhile, put the dripping into a large roasting tin and put it into the oven to heat until almost smoking. When the dripping is hot tip in all the vegetables, turning them over to coat them evenly with the dripping.

Replace the roasting tin in the oven and roast the vegetables, occasionally turning them over, for 35 to 40 minutes. When ready, they should be golden and tender. Serve immediately.

Gratin Dauphinoise

We make this delicious potato dish with just potatoes and cream; that is without cheese, garlic or bacon. You can add any of these if you wish – it's a matter of personal taste. It might be worth mentioning, however, that given half a chance and some truffle, we would not be shy of the addition of a few slivers to make it a truly luxurious dish.

800g Charlotte, La Ratte or another variety of firm potato, sliced
300ml single cream, or half and half double cream and milk
salt and pepper
50g butter

Preheat the oven to 200°C (400°F), Gas Mark 6.

Put the potatoes in a large saucepan with the cream or cream and milk, salt and pepper and bring to a simmer for about 5 minutes, stirring gently to prevent the potatoes sticking to the bottom of the pan. Butter a shallow 1.5-litre gratin dish with the 50g butter.

Transfer the potato slices to the dish, spreading them out evenly. Pour on the hot cream and put into the oven for about 1 hour. The top should be golden and bubbling. If you think it is getting too dry, cover with a piece of kitchen foil.

Chard Gratin

The name gratin comes from the French word gratte *– the crusty bits that stick to the sides of the baking dish. There is an almost inexhaustible supply of vegetables that are suitable for a gratin. Here's a basic recipe, using chard, both the stalks in their multi-coloured variety and the dark green, glossy leaves.*

a large bunch of chard
salt and white pepper
400ml milk
150ml single cream
100g butter
30g plain flour
a scrape of nutmeg
100g Parmesan cheese, grated

Preheat the oven to 220°C (425°F), Gas Mark 7.

Slice the chard stalks into 2.5 to 3 cm lengths, and chop the leaves. Blanch the leaves and stalks separately in boiling salted water for about 5 minutes, and then drain. Heat up the milk and cream to just below boiling point.

Melt half the butter in a roomy saucepan, then stir in the flour and allow the mixture to bubble for a minute or two. Slowly pour in the hot milk and cream, whisking while the liquid comes to a boil to make a thickish white sauce. Season with salt and white pepper and a scrape of nutmeg.

Butter a gratin dish with the remaining butter. Fold the chard into the sauce and tip it all into the gratin dish. Sprinkle the top with the Parmesan and put into the oven, or under a hot grill, for about 10 minutes until bubbling and golden.

Beans and Peas

Cooking French, green, or haricot beans inspires rather a lot of controversy – do you cook them al dente, until they squeak, or until they are mushy? We are firmly of the school that advocates that crunchy beans are unacceptable; however, cooking them until they are grey is equally horrid. Somewhere in between is the ideal, so careful watching of the pan is recommended.

When they are young, broad beans can be boiled and served in their outer skin; however, as the season progresses, the skin becomes rather tougher and the beans are best served slipped from the skins – rather a satisfying if laborious task.

Fresh, young peas need only the briefest cooking time, older peas somewhat more – again watching the pot; a slotted spoon at the ready for sporadic testing is useful. Add salt after cooking as it toughens the skins of peas and beans.

To butter or not to butter? It depends on what you are serving the vegetables with. If the dish has a creamy sauce then butter might be excessive, if it is a grill, or cold cuts, then buttering the beans or peas when they are hot would be entirely appropriate.

Kohl Rabi

A member of the brassica family, kohl rabi is delicious when really young. We take them from the garden when they are the size of table tennis balls. Sliced thinly and briefly cooked in boiling salted water until tender, their pale translucent green not only looks wonderful, but has a superb, delicate taste.

Young Courgettes, Chard Stems, Fennel, Baby Beetroot

Baby vegetables have a remarkable fresh flavour and texture that makes them perfect accompaniments to a summer meal. Young courgettes, chard stems, fennel, baby beetroot, cooked until just tender and buttered are simple and delicious.

Ratatouille

A summer vegetable stew that has almost as many recipes as there are cooks. Do you cook all the vegetables separately, mixing them at the final stage, or all together? Do you add green peppers? Do you cook it on top of the stove or in the oven? This is a recipe developed from experimentation and gives a rather nice firm ratatouille. It is better left for twenty-four hours before you eat it; the optimum temperature for serving is room temperature.

200ml olive oil
6 courgettes, sliced
3 onions, sliced
2 red peppers, cored, deseeded and sliced
2 aubergines, quartered and thickly sliced
4 garlic cloves, finely sliced
8 tomatoes, skinned, deseeded and quartered
salt and pepper
a large sprig of thyme
a bay leaf

Preheat the oven to 180°C (350°F), Gas Mark 4.

Heat half the oil in a large sauté pan and sauté the courgettes gently. When they have softened and are just starting to gild, transfer them to an ovenproof casserole, leaving as much oil as possible in the pan.

Put the onions into the sauté pan and cook gently until wilted. Put them with the courgettes. Sauté the red peppers in the hot oil until they have softened and add them to the casserole. Cook the aubergines in the pan – you may have to add some more oil – until they are just turning golden. Transfer to the casserole.

Gently sauté the garlic until it just turns transparent. Add the tomatoes to the pan. Season with salt and pepper and cook until the tomatoes have become very soft. Tip them over the vegetables in the casserole, together with the thyme and bay leaf, stirring gently to distribute the tomatoes among the vegetables. Cover with a lid and cook in the oven for 20 minutes. Take off the lid and cook for a further 35 minutes.

Add the remaining olive oil, allow to cool completely, then cover the casserole again and keep the ratatouille for 24 hours before you serve it at room temperature.

Celeriac Purée

Closely related to celery, celeriac has a more subtle and earthy flavour. It is a great winter vegetable – delicious roasted, grated and tossed in mustard mayonnaise, or puréed with potatoes.

800g celeriac, chopped
salt and white pepper
1 large potato, cubed
50g butter
50ml single cream

Boil the celeriac in plenty of salted water for 20 minutes. Add the potato into the boiling water and continue to cook for another 20 minutes until the celeriac and potato are tender.

Drain the vegetables well, returning them to the pan and shaking over a gentle heat until they have dried off a bit. Push the vegetables through a mouli-legumes or a potato ricer.

Heat up the butter and cream and stir into the purée, adding salt and white pepper to taste.

Ceps with Potatoes, Garlic and Parsley

The pungent flavour of Boletus edulus *– cèpe or porcini (cep or penny-bun) – seems to infuse potatoes when they are cooked together. Add some parsley and garlic, and you have a sublime dish. You can cheat a bit by adding a few sliced, firm, button mushrooms – they will take on the flavour of ceps during cooking.*

1kg potatoes – Pink Fir Apple, La Ratte or something else firm and waxy
salt and pepper
2 tablespoons good olive oil
250g fresh ceps, or as many as you can afford, thickly sliced
a handful of finely chopped parsley
2 garlic cloves, finely chopped

Boil the potatoes in their skins in plenty of salted water, until just cooked. Drain and when cool enough to handle, peel and thickly slice the potatoes .

Heat the oil in a shallow pan. Sauté the potatoes and mushrooms gently in the oil until the ceps begin to melt. Sprinkle with the parsley and garlic, shaking the pan to distribute them evenly, allowing the garlic to cook slightly.

Serve on very hot plates and eat very slowly, savouring each mouthful.

Wine with Food

A meal without wine is like a day without sun – dull. For this reason we have asked our friend Bill Baker to suggest plain, simple and modest wines to accompany our recipes. His advice will add pleasure to your meals and your life.

At the heart of *Classic Conran* is the sort of food one could expect to find in most French provincial towns. Unfortunately, the classic French wines that once accompanied them have become often prohibitively expensive. Formerly, the risk one ran in ordering a Puligny-Montrachet Folatières or a Volnay Caillerets was that the producer was either a charlatan or someone to whom the precious legacy of such a vineyard should not have been afforded; now the risk is more from impending bankruptcy. Nevertheless, France still offers wonderful, simple wines at reasonable prices. As with food, however, it is necessary to have a little basic knowledge of the people who make the wines.

Classic areas

Bordeaux

At the level of simple wines Bordeaux has to be said to be a difficult place to go looking. That said, one can find marvellous small wines from the more outlying areas: Lalande-de-Pomerol, Fronsac, Bourg and Blaye, the satellite areas of Saint-Emilion and even the lowly appellations labelled Bordeaux Supérieur. It is almost easier here to indicate what to avoid, namely blended wines with names like Baron de this or Comte de that; anything just labelled Bordeaux or anything from the *caves co-opératives*.

Burgundy – Red

Top wines from this area are so expensive that one must look away from its geographical epicentre. In the Côte Chalonnaise the three villages of Rully, Mercurey and Givry produce excellent, lightish Pinot Noir in the hands of producers like Faiveley, Yves de Suremain, Mouton, Jacquesson and Dureuil Janthial. To the north, the villages behind the main drag of the Côte d'Or – Auxey-Duresses, Pernand-Vergelesses, Saint Romain, Ladoix, Monthélie, Marsannay, Saint-Aubin and Chorey les Beaune still offer good value. Watch for growers like Chandon de Briailles, Tollot Beaut and Ampeau, and do not ignore merchants such as Jadot, Drouhin and Faiveley. Look for Bourgogne rouge wines from growers like Lafarge, Potel, Bachelet and Ghislaine Barthod; and Côte de Beaune, Côte de Nuits and Hautes-Côtes de Nuits wines from Jadot, Faiveley and the Gros family.

Finally, if you do want to spend a little more, Santenay and Savigny from growers like Pavelot and Colin, and merchants such as Girardin usually repay purchase.

Burgundy – White

Much of the advice for red Burgundy also applies to white. However, in the Côte Chalonnaise, one needs to add the village of Montagny. The more southerly vineyards of the Mâconnais (Mâcon and Saint-Véran, and the Fuissé appellations) produce some very serious whites. Look for growers like Lafon, Verget, Goyard, Vincent and Rijkeart.

In the Côte de Beaune the same villages are worth looking for as for their red wines. The vineyards of Saint-Aubin and Saint-Romain produce more white than red (look for the names of d'Allaines, Colin, and Hubert Lamy), but there are fewer whites than reds from Ladoix, Monthélie and Pernand-Vergelesses, where they exist they are often worth trying.

In Savigny and Santenay there is sensational value to be found from Jadot and especially from Girardin; some of his more expensive wines are quite oaky but at this level there is pure Chardonnay fruit.

It is strictly incorrect to lump Chablis in with white Burgundy, the vineyards being substantially to the north of the top end of the Côte d'Or. However, the wines are made of Chardonnay and thus bear a resemblance. They should not bear that much of a resemblance, though, and there has been much winemaking recently in Chablis, which relies heavily on oak, this rather ruins the delicate and individual minerality that the Chablis soils impart to the Chardonnay grape. It is this very minerality which one must search. Look for the wine of Brocard and Michel.

Beaujolais

Despite the gradually rising price of such wines as Fleurie, Moulin-a-Vent and Juliénas Beaujolais must feature in this list because its wines go so well with many of the recipes in *Classic Conran* – even with some of the fish dishes. Though Beaujolais-Villages can please, straight Beaujolais is best avoided. The villages which are permitted to name their wines are the best bet. Fleurie is the most popular, though often the most disappointing (look for the wines of André Colonge). Wines from Moulin-à-Vent, Morgon and Brouilly tend to be the biggest, while Chiroubles, St-Amour and Juliénas are usually the lightest of the region but have lovely raspberry Gamay fruit.

Rhône

The Rhône is quintessential territory for those looking for chunky, full-bodied red wines and there is still great value to be had. Basic Côtes-du-Rhône offers some real bargains. Guigal, the largest producer in the Rhône, makes a good example but there are dozens of others making great wines for sensible prices. Côtes-du-Rhône-Villages, which comprises seventeen villages in the southern Rhône, has some very serious up-and-coming domaines amongst which are Soumade, and Marcel Richaud whose Cairanne property produces consistently good wines each year. Lirac is still relatively little known and thus is a good source for Châteauneuf-like wines; the best address is the Domaine de la Mordorée.

If you are happy to pay a little more, choose from Gigondas (from Saint-Cosmé, Saint-Gayan and Raspail-Ay), Crozes-Hermitage (from Jaboulet, Chapoutier and Domaine des Remiziers), and Vacqueyras (Château des Tours and Clos de Cazaux). You can even venture into the now rather pricier areas like Châteauneuf-du-Pape, Saint-Joseph and Cornas – wonderful wines with game.

Loire

Who would have thought that Muscadet could undergo a rehabilitation – there is good wine here now and in general on the Loire. Crisp, clean Sauvignon wines from the vineyards of Sancerre and Pouilly-Fumé have become very expensive. Better value wines are to be had from the lesser-known nearby villages of Quincy, Reuilly and especially Ménétou Salon where Henri Pellé makes wines as good as any Sancerre (but sadly at the same price as the best Sancerre from such sources as Vacheron and Bourgeois, Delaporte and Mollet). Pouilly-Fumé, just across the river, makes wines at the same price level as Sancerre; there are several vineyards owned by various branches of the Dagueneau family all of which make excellent Sauvignon Blanc wines, the best but considerably the most expensive come from Didier.

The whites produced in the 'central section' of the Loire Touraine, Vouvray and Montlouis, are made with Chenin Blanc and are a more acquired taste but do try the wines of Huet in Vouvray – the dry (sec) versions are marvellous with river fish, and the sweeter ones deserve to be drunk by themselves or with ripe peaches.

Alsace

Alsace has changed hands between France and Germany four times since the end of the Franco-Prussian war in 1871. Until recently the wines were the only French wines named after grapes rather than villages. The Riesling is looked upon by the Alsatians as the king of grapes but it is the spicy Gewürztraminer that has found wider appeal. The real value, however, is in Pinot Blanc, which it is essential to drink while it is young and fresh.

Pinot Gris is an exciting grape in the right hands and is excellent with charcuterie, and especially with foie gras.

Alsace is simple in one way: know your growers and you usually get good wine. Look for Trimbach, Hugel, Schlumberger, Bott-Geyl, Boxler and Zind-Humbrecht. That said the sweetness levels of the various cuvées of these growers can be confusing. For the drier style go for Trimbach, for the luscious and concentrated use Zind-Humbrecht. Alsace wines make perfect aperitifs.

French Country Wines

It is in this catch-all, geographically indefinable area where the most advances have been made and where the most exciting wines at the best values are to be found. This is the source of the simple good value wines of France.

Provence

Bandol is possibly the most sophisticated of the southern appellations; it is made predominantly with Mourvèdre – strong and spicy, firm and long-lasting. Look for wines with a bit of age. The best producers are headed by Domaine Tempier and include Domaine Bunan and Château de Pibarnon. Bandol rosé wines are a great drink in the summer, and some of the whites can be good. Both whites and rosés, unlike the reds, should be drunk as early as possible in their lives.

The second most important area is the Côteaux d'Aix-en-Provence between Aix and Salon de Provence. There is a sub-section around the mediaeval village of Les Baux. The wines of this area fall into two distinct groups: those made for early drinking, which include the rosés (mostly best drunk in situ), and those which need aging and have Syrah and Cabernet Sauvignon as their main components. The outstanding example of these is the Domaine de Trevallon whose wines used to be great value but they have now such an international reputation that their prices have become stratospheric. Look instead for wines from Château de Bargemone, Château Vignaleure, Mas de la Dame, Mas Saint Berthe and Domaine de Terres Blanches. There are a few other wines from Provence that are worth noting: Domaine de Triennes from the Côteaux Varois; Domaine Rabiega, Domaine Gavoty and Domaine de la Courtade from the Côtes-de-Provence and the Château de Bellet from Bellet.

Languedoc-Roussillon

This is what the French call the *Midi* and is the home of most *vin ordinaire*. There has been much exciting and positive improvement here over the last two decades. The main red grape varieties used are Grenache, Syrah, Mourvèdre, Counoise, Carignan and Cinsault. (Southern French Mixture – SFM)

The Costières de Nimes produces good value reds from SFM and makes some decent rosés too. The best producers are Château de Belle-Coste, Château Mourges du Gres and Château de Saint-Cyrges. This is an area to watch as quality is very much on the up.

The Côteaux du Languedoc spreads over a huge tract of land in the Hérault but edges into both the Aude and the Gard, and is now a very complicated appellation with many geographical subsections although it is confined mainly to hillside sites. Pic Saint-Loup is the best subsection where Mas Bruguiere, Château de Lascaux and above all Domaine de l'Hortus are making excellent wines. Unusually, Hortus makes equally good white wines (the Grande Cuveé is half Chardonnay and half Viognier) as red (Syrah and Mouvèdre with about 15 per cent Grenache). There is a class act in Cabrieres, the Prieuré-de-St Jean de Bebian whose red wine is made from a third each Grenache, Mourvèdre and Syrah.

Another subsection worthy of mention is the area of Saint-Georges d'Orques on the edge of Montpelier, an area that has enjoyed a reputation and a documented export to the UK since 1715; the finest source is Domaine Henry.

In the Côteaux du Languedoc, at Saint-Saturnin near the village of Saint-Pargoire, the Domaine Peyre-Rose makes outstanding wine from Syrah with small amounts of Grenache or Mourvèdre depending upon the cuvée; it is among the longest-lived and greatest of the southern French wines. Finally, right on the coast Picpoul de Pinet is produced. This is a simple and yet satisfying summer drinking white when made by someone decent like the Domaine Felines-Jourdan. Picpoul means lip-stinger!

Faugères, in the foothills of the Cevennes, has been upgraded out of the Côteaux du Languedoc. This is wild country and the wines have the typical herby, piney flavour of the garrigue. Here the prime domaine is that of Jean Michel Alquier; it is expensive Faugères but worth paying for. The wines are dominated by Syrah.

St Chinian lies between Faugères and Minervois and was promoted to full appellation controllée in 1982. There is an increasing number of good growers and, unusually, two decent co-opératives. Unlike elsewhere there is nothing in the Appellation Contrôlée regulations to stop growers here making pure Syrah wine. Thus the wines are fuller than Minervois and less firm. Look for Château Cazal Viel and Domaine Borie la Vitarele.

Minervois is one of the oldest wine areas of France. Recently, the part called La Liviniere has been given its own AC and is a name to go for. There are many growers of note: Château de Gourgazaud, Château Coupe Roses, Domaine Lapeyre, Château d'Oupia and Domaine Borie de Maurel whose Cuvée Scylla is one of the very top wines from the Midi. Minervois and its close neighbour Corbières have roots in Phoencian times. Corbières is the biggest vineyard in Languedoc and its size, different micro-climates and soils make it impossible to make sweeping statements about the quality or weight of the wines produced. That said, the wines seem to be drier and less sophisticated than many of the nearby areas. There is good wine at great value to be found from properties such as Château de Lastours, Château Voulte-Gasparets, and Château les Ollieux Romanis.

The best traditionally-made Côtes du Roussillon and Côtes du Rousillon-Villages are worth a mention. There is still a great deal of Carignan, a grape rather frowned upon by modernists but one which, when given very old vines can make a significant contribution to the wines from the south. A maximum of 60 per cent is allowed here with a minimum of 20 per cent Syrah and Mourvèdre. Look for Domaine Gauby, Domaine Cazes and Château Rozes.

The South West

This winemaking in this part of France has moved forward apace in the last ten or so years. The most important appellation here is Madiran. Alain Brumont (who owns the best property, Chateau Montus) and two others, Meinjarre and Bouscasse, really pushed the area back into production. Along with Brumont the following are worth looking for; Domaine Chapelle Lenclos, Chateau d'Aydie and Chateau Barrejat. White wine is produced in the area under the label Pacherenc du Vic-Bilh (improbable but true). Some is made with Gros & Petit Manseng, some, like Brumont's Chateau Bouscasse with Corbu only. These can be refreshing and fascinating wines.

Irouleguy is mostly a red wine but some good whites do exist – I have never had a decent rose. The reds are from Tannat like at Madiran but again like there Cabernet Sauvignon and Cabernet Franc are often adjuncts. The best producer is probably Domaine Ilarria whose Cuvée Bixintxo is outstanding Tannat. Domaine Brana make good wine as well and they also make very good Poire William.

Jurancon is entirely white wine made from Gros and Petit Manseng. Until relatively recently this was an area which only made sweet wines – these are well worth looking out for but the best have become very pricey. The dry wines are crisp, clean and very individual. Look for Domaine Cauhape, Domaine Ramonteu, Clos Guirouilh, Clos Lapeyre and Clos Uroulat.

Around Bordeaux

Bergerac is the area closest to Bordeaux. The wine is made with the same grapes as Bordeaux: Cabernet Sauvignon, Cabernet Franc and Merlot. White and rosé wines are also made; the best sources are Château Tour des Gendres, Château la Jaubertie and Château Pique Segue. The red wines are lighter than those of Bordeaux. The white wines are mostly crisp and quite obviously Sauvignon.

The nearby Côtes de Duras makes white and red wines. The whites are better than the reds and the best producer is the Domaine de Laulan, which produces a Loire-like Sauvignon. Also close by are the vineyards of Monbazillac and Saussignac, where sweet wines are made. Saussignac has rather overtaken Monbazillac on quality and is very good value; look for the wine of Château les Eyssards.

Cahors

The grape grown here is the tough, tannic Malbec. Recent planting of Merlot in the area has gone some way to softening it. Nevertheless, if you go for wines from the best domaines with a little age there are rewards to be had. The best is Clos Triguedina whose Cuvée Prince Probus is probably the best wine of the area. Other producers to watch are Clos Gamot and Château Lagrezette.

2000
MONOPOLE
APPELLATION

Puddings

While we rarely eat pudding when eating on our own, entertaining family or friends always provides a good excuse to make one. Invariably our puddings are fruit-based. Spring brings rhubarb and early gooseberries, so compotes, crumbles and pies are made. During the summer we choose soft fruits – strawberries, blackcurrants, redcurrants and, later, raspberries. We serve them as summer pudding, Eton mess, jellies or just on their own with thick Jersey cream. When we have the bounty of the orchard – apples, pears and, periodically, quinces – we make pies, tarts and compotes, poached pears, baked apples and quince jellies. Of course there is sometimes room for comforting rice pudding, bread and butter pudding or steamed pudding with custard. Occasionally an elegant pudding is called for and crème brûlée, îles flottantes or rich chocolate mousse generally fits the bill. Again when choosing your pudding, think about what precedes it and choose something that complements your main course without overpowering your appetite.

Gooseberry fool

Something to look forward to at the beginning of the summer, those first green and sharp gooseberries, puréed and folded into creamy custard. Other fruits work too, but there's something about the gooseberry that is the quintessential foolish fruit.

500g young gooseberries, topped and tailed
50g butter
3 egg yolks
50g caster or granulated sugar
250ml cream

Put the gooseberries into a stainless or enamelled pan with the butter and heat gently, shaking the pan to prevent the fruit sticking. When the gooseberries have softened and started to collapse, mash them roughly with a potato masher. If you want a smooth purée, push it through a mouli-legumes.

Meanwhile, beat the egg yolks with the sugar in a basin. Heat the cream in a small saucepan until just below boiling point. While whisking, pour the cream on to the egg yolks and place the basin over a pan of simmering water. Stir until the custard thickens, then allow to cool, stirring from time to time to prevent a skin forming.

When both the gooseberries and custard are cool, combine them then chill until you want to eat the fool.

You can add some elderflower syrup in place of the sugar, which gives a subtle flavour that is entirely compatible with the gooseberries.

Rhubarb Compote

500g pink forced rhubarb, cut into 3 to 4cm sticks
50g butter
50g sugar
a piece of fresh ginger, grated – optional

Preheat the oven to 180°C (350°F) Gas Mark 4.

Lay the rhubarb in a buttered gratin dish, and sprinkle with sugar, and the grated ginger, if using. Put in the oven for about 30 minutes until soft but still intact.

Take the dish from the oven and allow the rhubarb to cool.

Fruit Crumble

Comforting and delicious, rhubarb, gooseberry or apple crumble, though reminiscent of school, is always popular. The secret is to use a lot of butter and sugar which form a sort of toffee-biscuity crumble.

130g plain flour
100g butter – cold and grated
50g brown sugar
50g caster sugar
750g prepared fruit

Preheat the oven to 190°C (375°F), Gas Mark 5.

Sift the flour into a bowl and add the butter. Very lightly rub the butter into the flour. Stir in the sugars and put the bowl into the fridge while you prepare the fruit.

Liberally butter a 1 litre pie or gratin dish and put in the fruit – rhubarb needs no cooking, gooseberries or apples need softening a bit beforehand. Sprinkle on the crumble and bake for 25 to 30 minutes, until the pudding is bubbling around the edges and golden on top.

Serve with cream, or custard for that authentic school dining-room experience.

Fruit Jelly

Not quite the wobbly, hundreds-and-thousands-scattered pudding of children's parties, this is rather more adult. Blackcurrant jelly has been a perennially popular pudding on the menu at Bibendum in London's Fulham Road, where it is served with warm madeleines. We make jelly using the lovely pink early rhubarb and serve it with rhubarb compote. The method can be used for other fruit too – raspberries and strawberries in the summer, citrus fruits in the winter.

500g rhubarb, chopped into pieces
200g caster sugar
4 gelatine leaves – about 12.5g

Put the rhubarb pieces into a stainless or enamelled saucepan. Add a splash of water to stop it sticking to the pan and heat very gently to simmering point. Allow to simmer for 15 minutes, breaking up the rhubarb with a wooden spoon.

Suspend a jelly bag (or a strainer lined with two layers of muslin) over a bowl and transfer the rhubarb to the bag, allowing the juice to drip through without encouraging it in any way, for at least 6 hours or overnight.

Discard the solids in the jelly bag or muslin and measure the resulting liquid. Add enough water to make it up to 500ml. Pour the juice into a pan, add the sugar, then set over a gentle heat to dissolve the sugar.

Meanwhile, soak the gelatine leaves in cold water until they are soft, then add them to the rhubarb juice and stir to dissolve. On no account must the mixture boil. Remove from the heat and pour into a wetted mould, individual ramekins or dariole moulds. Allow to cool then refrigerate until set.

Dipping the moulds into hot water makes it easy to turn out the jellies. Make sure, however, that the serving plates are well chilled.

Eton mess

There seems to be some argument as to whether this was a pudding invented by the eponymous college. It doesn't really matter how it came into being, it is one of the finest, and indeed most simple of puddings.

500g strawberries, sliced
50g vanilla sugar
500ml double cream, chilled
4 x 10 to 15cm meringues (see below), broken into pieces

Place the strawberries in a glass or ceramic bowl and dredge with the vanilla sugar.

Pour the cream into the bowl in which you want to serve the pudding and beat it until it is lightly whipped.

Fold the strawberries and meringues into the cream – it should be faintly marbled. Serve immediately.

Meringues

This recipe will make more than you need for Eton mess, but meringue keeps very well, wrapped in tissue paper, in a cake tin.

6 egg whites
a pinch of salt
a pinch of cream of tartar
350g caster sugar

Preheat the oven to about 110°C (225°F), Gas Mark ¼. Line a large baking sheet with non-stick baking parchment.

Beat the egg whites, salt and cream of tartar in a large bowl until the whites are stiff, but not too dry and holey. While beating allow 250g of the sugar to drift on to the whites and continue to beat until the mixture is stiff and glossy. Fold in the remaining sugar.

Place large spoonfuls of the meringue on the baking sheet, making them round, oval or whatever shape takes your fancy. You can make a large pavlova if you want. Place the baking sheet in the oven for 1 hour.

Take a look and see if the meringues are sufficiently dry – if not, leave them for another 30 minutes.

Remove the meringues from the oven and transfer them to a wire rack to cool.

Compote of Apples

This is a great standby pudding, especially during the autumn glut of apples. You can also use pears, stone fruits or dried fruits such as apricots and prunes. If you are lucky enough to have access to quinces, they impart a wonderful flavour to apple or pear compote. You can flavour the cooking syrup, too, with citrus peel, vanilla beans, raisins, cinnamon sticks, cloves or other spices.

8 dessert apples
the juice of a lemon
350g caster or granulated sugar
600ml water

Peel, core and quarter the apples and sprinkle with lemon juice.

Meanwhile, put the sugar and water and whatever flavouring you might wish into a large stainless steel or enamelled pan, heat gently to dissolve the sugar, then bring to the boil. Add the apples and poach them in the syrup until they are tender.

Different varieties of apples cook in different ways – some stay firm and become transparent, others become floury and break up – so it's worth keeping an eye on the fruit as it cooks.

Transfer the apples and the syrup to a bowl and allow to cool.

Serve the compote at room temperature or chilled with cream.

If you make a compote using dried fruits, you will have to soak them before you poach them in the syrup.

Baked Apples

50g walnuts, coarsely chopped
50g currants
50g brown sugar
4 cooking apples, cored
juice of 1 lemon
50g butter

Preheat the oven to 200°C (400°F), Gas Mark 6.

Mix together the walnuts, currants and 1 teaspoon of the brown sugar and press into the space left by the apple cores.

Liberally butter an ovenproof baking dish large enough to hold the apples.

Place the stuffed apples in the buttered dish and sprinkle them with any left-over currants or nuts, the remaining sugar and the lemon juice. Put a smear of butter on each of the apples and place the dish in the oven for about 1 hour, until a skewer goes through the apples with no resistance. Basting the apples with the juices from time to time.

Serve warm, with lots of cold cream.

Tarte Tatin

You tend to see all sorts of variations of Tarte Tatin – pear, tomato, chicory – on fashionable restaurant menus. While this sort of inventiveness is not to be dismissed out of hand, the original, made famous by the Tatin sisters who ran the restaurant in Lamotte-Beuvron (a small village south of the Loire), is still the best. Use a pan that can go on top of the stove as well as in the oven – we make it in a nice shallow copper frying pan.

150g granulated sugar
150g butter
800g apples, peeled and cored – dessert varieties work best
300g pastry – traditionally shortcrust, though we use butter puff pastry

Tarte Tatin is traditionally served at warmish room temperature with plenty of cream.

Melt the sugar in a shallow 30cm-wide pan that can also go in the oven. When the sugar starts to caramelise, add the butter and continue to cook it until it becomes a sort of toffee. Take the pan off the heat.

Keeping one apple half, cut the rest of the apples into quarters. Put the half in the centre of the pan, cut side up, and then the quarters arranged round it, quite closely packed. Cook the apples for a bit on a low heat, without moving them, until they are caramel-coloured and have soaked up the butter. Allow the apples to cool completely.

Preheat the oven to 200°C (400°F), Gas Mark 6.

Roll out the pastry to a circle and lay it over the apples. Tuck it down the inside of the pan to seal in the apples. Bake for 20–30 minutes.

Allow the tart to cool in the pan for about 5–10 minutes before you turn it out on to a plate.

500g
AVERY

Summer Pudding

This is such an impressive pudding – it always generates exclamations of admiration – and it is so easy. It is regarded as a special treat because the season when you can make it is relatively short. Do try to get decent bread – standard white, sliced sandwich loaf tends to be rather slimy. Brioches give an interesting if unauthentic texture.

1 small loaf of white bread, crusts removed, and sliced
1kg summer fruits – redcurrants, blackcurrants, raspberries, and strawberries
200g caster sugar

Line the bottom of a 2-litre pudding basin with a circle of bread, then line the sides with slices cut to fit nice and neatly. Reserve a couple of slices for the top.

Strip the redcurrants and blackcurrants from their stalks and put them into a large stainless steel or enamelled pan together with the raspberries and strawberries, halved if large, and the sugar. Heat slowly until the juice starts to run, stirring it gently. Remove the pan from the heat – you don't want the fruit to collapse to a mush. Spoon the fruit into the basin with the juice – fill it right to the top.

Cover the basin with bread to make a neat seal. Put a saucer or plate just small enough to fit inside the basin on top. Weigh the saucer down with some weights, cans of tomatoes or something else heavy and, placing the basin on a dish to catch any overflow, refrigerate overnight.

The pudding can happily live in the fridge for a couple of days.

When you want to unmould it, run the blade of a thin knife round the edge and invert the pudding over the serving dish. A couple of shakes should successfully coax the pudding out of the basin.

Serve with lots of thick cream.

Poached Pears

A very simple yet pretty pudding, it is especially good in the winter – you cook the pears in what is essentially mulled wine. The pudding only needs lashing of thick cream. Oh, and a crystallised violet.

4 pears
½ bottle of robust red wine
½ cinnamon stick
2 cloves
a scrape of nutmeg
a strip of orange rind
1 tablespoon redcurrant jelly
150g brown sugar
4 crystallized violets (optional)

Preheat the oven to 150°C (300°F), Gas Mark 2.

Peel the pears, but leave the stalks on. Put them and all the other ingredients into a flameproof casserole with a lid. Bring to a simmer, cover, then place in the oven for 2 hours.

If you can, leave the pears in the poaching liquor in a cool place overnight. Remove the pears to a serving plate or bowl, and return the casserole to the heat. Boil to reduce the liquid until it has reached a syrupy consistency. Strain it over the pears, which should now look glossy garnet-red.

If you have some, a crystallized violet on each pear looks marvellous, but that's just a bit of whimsy and they're equally delicious without.

Christmas Pudding

We always think it totally inappropriate to eat Christmas pudding after such a rich and filling meal as the full Christmas dinner. It's the last thing you feel like eating. We generally eat the pudding a couple of days later, having eaten something more modest beforehand. We don't like raisins so tend to use extra currants and prunes to make up the amounts. It's a bit of a myth that you need to make Christmas pudding weeks ahead – twenty-four hours is perfectly all right. It's just convenient to get the preparation done during a less frantic time of year.

Makes 2 large puddings, each feeding at least 6 to 8 people.

225g sultanas
225g currants
115g pitted prunes, chopped
115g candied peel, chopped – the good stuff
115g blanched almonds, chopped
225g dark demerara sugar
225g fresh breadcrumbs
115g plain flour
1 teaspoon mixed spice
a big scrape of nutmeg
225g shredded suet, or grated butter
4 large eggs, beaten
150ml stout
100ml brandy
Cognac, to serve

Mix the dry ingredients and the suet or butter in a huge bowl.

Stir the eggs and stout together, pour on to the dry ingredients and mix very well; traditionally everyone in the household should have a stir (and a wish). Allow the mixture to soak for 24 hours then stir in the brandy.

Spoon the mixture into two buttered 1.5-litre pudding basins. Cover the basins with a double thickness of greaseproof paper – pleated to allow for expansion – and tie with string.

Bring two large pans of water to a vigorous boil, lower the basins into the water, cover and steam for 5 hours, topping up the water with boiling water as necessary. Remove the basins from the water and leave the puddings to cool. Store in a cold place.

On the day you want to eat the pudding, renew the cover and steam for 2 to 3 hours.

To serve the pudding, turn it out of the basin on to a heated serving plate, warm a measure of Cognac, turn down the lights and demand a hush among your diners. Pour the Cognac over the pudding and set a match to it.

The traditional accompaniment to Christmas pudding is brandy butter, but we prefer really cold, yellow Jersey cream.

Steamed Ginger Pudding

Redolent of school dinners, steamed puddings nearly always inspire derogatory comments – the association with lumpy custard is probably in some way responsible. This pudding is quite light and grown up, and deliciously satisfying on a winter's day. Preserved ginger is easy to get and makes the pudding far more luxurious than when made with dry ground ginger, though a pinch of it in the mix does give a bit of a hit.

20ml ginger syrup from the jar of preserved ginger (below)
100g butter
100g caster sugar
2 eggs, beaten
125g preserved ginger, chopped into small dice
125g self-raising flour
a pinch of ground ginger
150ml milk

Butter a 2-litre pudding basin and pour in the ginger syrup, tipping the bowl to coat the sides a bit. Place a trivet or a saucer in the base of a saucepan, half fill it with water and bring it to a vigorous boil.

Meanwhile, cream the butter and sugar together until light and fluffy, then add the eggs and preserved ginger.

Fold in the flour and ground ginger, slackening the mixture with the cold milk.

Turn the mixture into the pudding basin, tie a double thickness of buttered greaseproof paper over the top and put into the saucepan. Turn the water down to a simmer after 10 minutes and cook for 2 hours, checking the water level from time to time; if it appears to be boiling dry, add more boiling water.

When the pudding is cooked, turn it out on to a serving dish.

Really cold, thick cream is particularly good with this, though the more abstemious may prefer egg custard.

Crème Caramel

125g caster sugar
550ml creamy milk
25g vanilla sugar
4 eggs

Preheat the oven to 160°C (325°F), Gas Mark 3.

If you are brave enough, put the caster sugar into a heavy-based pan and let it melt over a gentle heat, then turn the heat up and cook the sugar until it is the caramel you like. Otherwise dissolve the sugar in 100ml water and boil it until the caramel stage is reached.

Quickly pour the caramel into a baking dish – a 1-litre soufflé dish is ideal.

Heat the milk with the vanilla sugar in a small saucepan until just below boiling. Beat the eggs in a basin, add the milk, whisking vigorously, and strain though a conical sieve on to the caramel. Put the baking dish into a roasting tin half-filled with boiling water and place it in the oven for about 1 hour, after which the custard should be set.

Remove the dish from the tin and allow the custard to cool, then refrigerate for at least 12 hours.

When you want to serve the crème caramel, turn it out on to a serving dish. The custard will have a lovely caramel sauce running over it.

Rice Pudding

Another staple of the nursery repertoire. You can use 'pudding' rice, but we find short-grained risotto rice, vialone nano or arborio, gives a subtle flavour to an otherwise rather bland pudding. You can, of course, spice it up with orange or lemon rind or indeed spices such as cinnamon or nutmeg. One of the best parts of this pudding is the crusty bits that are left clinging to the edge of the baking dish, something that's hotly fought over in our household.

50g short-grain rice
550ml creamy milk
30g sugar
1 tablespoon butter

Preheat the oven to 180°C (350°F), Gas Mark 4.

Put the rice, milk and sugar into a saucepan, and simmer gently for 5 minutes.

Generously butter a shallow baking dish. Pour the hot, milky rice into the baking dish and dot the butter on the surface. Put into the oven for 1 hour, stirring after 20 minutes. There should be a lovely golden skin on the surface and creamy rice underneath when it is cooked.

Serve hot or warm with cold cream and perhaps a bit of damson jam.

Iles Flottantes

300ml milk
200ml cream
1 vanilla pod, split lengthways
6 egg yolks
200g vanilla sugar
6 egg whites
200g caster sugar

For the caramel:
4 tablespoons caster sugar

Preheat the oven to 140°C (275°F), Gas Mark 1.

Bring the milk and cream, with the vanilla pod, to a boil and remove from the heat.

Meanwhile, beat the egg yolks with the vanilla sugar in a large bowl, then pour on the milk and cream, having first removed the vanilla pod (if you like the custard with black speckles, scrape the seeds out with the tip of a knife).

Place the bowl over a pan of simmering water and stir until the mixture has thickened to a custard.

Pour the custard into a wide serving dish, allow to cool, cover the surface with clingfilm then put in the fridge.

In a really clean bowl, whisk the egg whites until they are white and foamy, then add the sugar a little bit at a time until the whites are firm and glossy. Pile them into a basin, cover loosely with a piece of silicone paper and place in a roasting tin filled with boiling water. Put the tin into the oven for 45 minutes until the meringue has set.

Remove from the oven and allow to cool; it will sink back a bit.

When the custard is cold, carefully remove the clingfilm and invert the meringue into the middle of the pool of custard.

To make the caramel, heat the caster sugar in a small saucepan until it has caramelised, then drizzle it liberally over the meringue.

A delicious alternative to caramel is praline (see page 227), which can be generously sprinkled over the meringue before serving.

Crème Brûlée

We make this in one large, shallow gratin dish – that way you get the right balance of cream and crisp. Use vanilla sugar, or add vanilla essence to the cream and use regular sugar. We're not great devotees of having the cream stiff with black vanilla seeds, they generally settle on the bottom and look alarmingly like cigarette ash. We have never found a domestic grill sufficiently hot to caramelize the sugar on top without further cooking the custard, resulting in an unsatisfactory texture. Buy a small blowtorch – they are not expensive, readily available from most DIY suppliers and great fun to use. There's always a fight for the blowtorching position in our house, rendering crème brûlée one of the most popular of puddings.

500ml cream
6 egg yolks
50g vanilla sugar
caster sugar, for dredging

Preheat the oven to 140°C (275°F), Gas Mark 1.

Put the cream into a non-stick saucepan and heat gently to simmering point.

Beat the egg yolks and vanilla sugar in a large bowl until well amalgamated. Pour the hot cream onto the egg mixture, stirring it vigorously. Pour through a fine sieve into a shallow gratin dish and place in a baking tin of boiling water. Place in the oven for about 45 minutes.

Remove the gratin dish from the baking tin, and allow to cool.

About 1 hour before serving, dredge a fine layer of caster sugar over the top of the custard and flame it with a blowtorch until you have a nice crisp caramel top.

Bread and Butter Pudding

A nursery staple that remains a favourite when one has grown up. Bread and butter pudding has grown up rather too, with the introduction of different breads – brioche and panettone are delicious – and marmalade, chocolate or other exotic ingredients being used in lieu of the traditional currants. Here is the basic recipe; you can tweak it according to your fancy.

60g butter
50g currants
4 slices of good white bread, crusts off, thickly buttered
550ml milk – full fat
50g vanilla sugar
2 large eggs
a scrape of nutmeg

Rub the butter liberally over the inside of an ovenproof gratin dish and sprinkle on a few currants. Cut the bread into triangles, squares, fingers, whatever, and lay them overlapping in the dish, sprinkling alternately with currants.

Warm the milk in a small saucepan. Lightly mix together the sugar and eggs in a basin and then pour on the hot milk, mixing it well. Strain through a conical sieve onto the bread and currants. Scrape a bit of nutmeg over the top. Leave to rest for about 30 minutes.

Preheat the oven to 180°C (350°F), Gas Mark 4. Put the pudding into the oven for 45 minutes until it has puffed up, the custard has set and the top is nicely golden.

Serve with very cold pouring cream.

Praline

200g blanched almonds
200g caster sugar

Preheat the grill. Oil a slab of marble or line a baking sheet with silicone paper.

Toast the almonds until they are nicely brown but not at all burned.

Put the sugar into a heavy-based pan and heat gently until the sugar has melted, then turn up the heat and cook until the sugar turns into a caramel. Tip in the almonds and mix together quickly.

Pour the praline mixture on to the oiled marble or silicone paper and allow it to cool completely.

Break up the praline and pound it to a fine granulation in a pestle and mortar or a food processor, or wrap it in a tea towel and pound it with a rolling pin.

Praline keeps very well in a polythene bag in the freezer.

Vanilla Ice Cream

This is the favourite all-round ice cream that goes with anything.

300ml milk
200ml double cream
1 vanilla pod, split lengthways
6 egg yolks
200g vanilla sugar

Bring the milk and cream, with the vanilla pod, to a boil, then remove from the heat.

Meanwhile, beat the egg yolks with the vanilla sugar in a large heatproof bowl, then pour on the milk and cream, having first removed the vanilla pod (if you like the custard with black speckles scrape the seeds out with the tip of a knife). Place the bowl over a sauce pan of simmering water and stir well until the mixture has thickened to a custard.

Pour the custard into a freezer-proof dish and chill.

Place the dish in the freezer and allow the custard to freeze until ice crystals form around the edges; this takes about 30 minutes, though the time depends on the temperature of the freezer.

With a fork break up the crystals and mix them into the unfrozen ice cream. Return the dish to the freezer and continue to break up the crystals every 20 minutes or so until the ice cream is solid. Then cover and freeze until required.

Chocolate Mousse

The simplest of puddings and wickedly full of chocolate. Use the very best possible chocolate and good eggs and you can't go wrong.

Per person:

25g plain chocolate (70% cocoa solids)
10g butter
1 egg, separated

Break up the chocolate and put it, with the butter, into a large basin and put that over a pan of hot, but not boiling, water and allow it to melt without stirring it.

When the mixture is completely molten remove the bowl from the heat, allow to cool slightly then add the egg yolks to the chocolate. You can stir it now.

Whisk the egg whites in a large, very, very clean basin until they have expanded and are quite stiff. Stir a tablespoonful of the egg white into the chocolate mixture to slacken it a bit, then very lightly and gently fold in the rest of the whites.

Coax the mixture into the serving dish or bowl, cover with clingfilm and refrigerate. It'll taste better the next day.

Add a splash of something alcoholic to the melted chocolate, if you wish to make it even more wicked.

Cheese

The cheese course can seem like a wasted element of a meal, served when we rarely feel like eating any more. How much better to have cheese as the principal dish of a meal? There is such a remarkable variety available that one could eat a different cheese every day for several years and still not exhaust the list. In his seminal work *The French Cheese Book*, Patrick Rance named 750 varieties of French cheese.

Farmhouse cheeses are really worth seeking out, those made carefully by craftsmen, in controllable amounts, properly matured and of a consistent quality. Specialist cheese shops will sell only those cheeses they are sure of, where they know the maker and supplier. They tend to be seasonal, brie is best in the spring, Saint-Marcellin during the summer, Vacherin peaks during the winter. Italian Parmesan and Pecorino, Spanish Manchego, and most English cheeses are good all year round.

Properly made, farmhouse cheeses tend to be a little more expensive than the pre-packed varieties, but they are really worth it. French cheeses are among the best in the world. Again look for the unpasturised *lait cru* varieties of Camembert, Brie and Vacherin, and you will be rewarded with a cheese that is very different from the mass-produced form of the same cheese. An aged Parmesan or Manchego Veijo, are an excellent addition to a cheese board, particularly when served with quince paste, membrillo.

When you buy cheese, buy just enough for your immediate needs – they don't keep very well. If you do need to store cheese, such as Parmesan, for example, wrap it in damp greaseproof paper and keep it somewhere cool, a fridge is not ideal, being rather too cold. Serve cheese with bread, biscuits, dried fruits, walnuts or just with a knife, fork and a glass of wine.

When you are serving cheese, choose a selection of three or four, any more tends to be confusing. Try and mix the types, one hard, one creamy, one blue and one fresh, goaty cheese.

Cheese we love include: Parmesan, Cheddar, Lancashire, Swaledale, Cheshire, Wensleydale, Roquefort, Oxford Blue, Emmenthal, Gruyère, Provolone, Fontina, Munster, Port Salut, Reblochon, Livarot, Vacherin Mont d'Or, Epoisses, Brie, Camembert, Gorgonzola, Saint-Marcellin, Pecorino, Cabécou, Feta and many, many more.

PETIT REBLOCHON J. GENANS
AU LAIT CRU
EMB. EDELMONT

Sandwiches

A prawn sandwich worth as much as a diamond ring? Well one might agree if it were a cucumber or egg-and-cress sandwich. Or truffle paste on a bridge roll. Or a *sandwich au jambon* and *une pression* in a Paris café. Who doesn't like sandwiches? It is said that those masters of the universe who travel regularly by Concorde eat sandwiches on board, shunning the more elaborate (and often overly-ambitious) fare offered by the airline. While travelling on a domestic flight within Germany, Lufthansa offered us the ideal refreshment – a brown roll filled with good German sausage and mustard, and a bottle of beer – delicious.

The important thing to remember when making sandwiches is their fitness for the occasion. Great doorsteps or chip butties are not entirely fitting for an elegant afternoon tea, and dainty morsels that wouldn't fill a fly would be completely out of place in a working lunch box.

Bread also plays its part – white for cucumber, brown for smoked salmon, baguette for ham, rye for salt beef… Crusts on or off? Whatever bread you prefer, the sandwich must be filled to the edge – there's little worse than a heap of filling in the centre and a desert round the edges. The filling must be prepared with the intention of filling a sandwich – as Oscar Wilde said, 'When I ask for a watercress sandwich, I do not mean a loaf with a field in the middle of it'.

A steak sandwich is a wonderful treat, however if you have to wrestle with a large piece of meat, it loses its appeal – slice the steak into manageable pieces before filling the roll.

An important thing, too, is that slippery fillings must be anchored within by another ingredient that has more purchase. The Club sandwich, hero of the hotel lobby menu, if not carefully constructed, can result in a large smear of mayonnaise-covered tomato decorating one's lap.

Scones

225g self-raising flour
1 teaspoon bicarbonate of soda
1 teaspoon salt
50g butter
150ml buttermilk
1 egg, beaten

Preheat the oven to 200°C (400°F), Gas Mark 6. Put a baking sheet into the oven to heat up.

Sift the flour into a basin with the bicarbonate of soda and salt and quickly and lightly rub in the butter.

Stir in the buttermilk with a palette knife. The less you work the dough the lighter the scones will be. Transfer the dough to a floured pastry board and press it out to about 3cm thick – you can use a rolling pin but the flat of the hand does just as well. Cut 5.5cm circles, re-rolling the scraps. Or, if you prefer, cut the dough into triangles or even squares.

Take the baking sheet from the oven and put the scones on to the hot surface, touching each other as this helps them to rise. Brush the surface with a little beaten egg and put the scones in the oven. They should take 10 to 12 minutes to rise and turn golden brown.

Cool the scones on a wire rack and try to resist eating them until they are warm – too hot and they'll burn your lips.

Flapjacks

This recipe makes thin, crisp flapjacks. If you prefer them thicker and chewy, bake them in a smaller tin.

125g butter
125g brown sugar
250g golden syrup
a squeeze of lemon juice
250g jumbo oats

Preheat the oven to 160°C (325°F), Gas Mark 3.

Melt the butter, brown sugar and golden syrup together in a large saucepan. When thoroughly mixed, add the lemon juice and the oats, stirring well.

Tip the flapjack mixture into a shallow 20 x 30cm shallow baking tin, pressing into the corners and levelling the surface. Put the tin in the oven for 30 to 40 minutes until the surface of the mixture is golden.

Take the tin from the oven and allow it to stand for 10 minutes, then, with a sharp knife, cut the flapjacks into squares, rectangles or whatever shape takes your fancy, leaving them in the tin to cool.

When the flapjacks are quite cool, they should break apart easily.

Banana Teabread

2 ripe bananas
1 egg
170g self-raising flour
½ teaspoon salt
a scrape of nutmeg
a pinch of ground cinnamon
50g chopped walnuts
100g vanilla sugar
25g butter, melted

Preheat the oven to 180°C (350°F), Gas Mark 4.

Mash the bananas with the egg in a shallow bowl. Sift the flour, salt, nutmeg and cinnamon together into a large bowl. Stir in the walnuts and vanilla sugar. Beat the banana and egg mixture into the flour, together with the melted butter.

Turn the cake mixture into a greased and lined small loaf tin (20 x 10 x 6cm). Bake for about 1 hour.

Allow the teabread to cool in the tin for 5 minutes, then turn it out onto a wire rack to cool completely.

Banana teabread will keep for up to one week if wrapped in film or foil, and stored in an airtight tin.

Lemon Cake

125g butter
175g caster sugar
½ teaspoon salt
grated rind of 2 lemons
2 eggs, beaten
175g self-raising flour

For the syrup:
juice of 2 lemons
75g icing sugar

Preheat the oven to 180°C (350°F), Gas Mark 4.

Cream the butter and sugar together in a large bowl. Add the salt and lemon rind, then the beaten eggs, a little at a time, beating well to keep the mixture light and fluffy; if it curdles, add a spoonful of flour.

Sift the self-raising flour onto the mixture and fold in. Turn into a greased and lined 20cm cake tin and bake for 45 minutes, until golden.

Meanwhile, make the syrup by gently heating the lemon juice with the icing sugar in a small pan.

When the cake is cooked, leave it in the tin and, with a toothpick or fine skewer, make several holes in the surface. Pour on the hot syrup, allowing it to soak into the cake. You may be alarmed by how much syrup there is, but it will soak in. Allow the cake to cool completely in the tin, then turn it out.

The cake will keep for up to a week in an airtight container.

Brown Soda Bread

This recipe is a favourite not just for the lovely comforting bread that never fails, but also for the instant gratification – you can have a loaf in about half an hour, something you can't achieve with yeast breads.

350g brown wholemeal stone-ground flour
220g plain white flour
1 teaspoon salt
1 teaspoon bicarbonate of soda
20g butter
300ml buttermilk

Preheat the oven to 230°C (450°F), Gas Mark 8. Put a baking sheet into the oven to heat up. Sift the flours, salt and bicarbonate of soda into a large basin and mix well. Rub in the butter, then, using a palette knife mix in the buttermilk. You should have a soft, not sticky, dough.

Flour a board and turn the dough out, kneading it very lightly. Shape it into a flattish round and cut a cross into the surface. Place the loaf onto the hot baking sheet and bake in the oven for 10 minutes. Turn the heat down to 200°C (400°F), Gas Mark 6 and cook for a further 15 minutes. To test whether the bread is done, tap the base with your finger. When ready it should make a hollow sound.

Set the loaf aside to cool. It is also delicious hot and buttered, although it tends to be crumbly when it is very fresh.

It will keep for 4 or 5 days if wrapped in greaseproof paper and kept in a cool place.

When preparing the dough for Brown Soda Bread, use a palette knife to mix together the sifted flours, salt, bicarbonate of soda, butter and buttermilk. Once the dough has formed, flour a board and turn the dough out, kneading it very lightly. Shape it into a flattish round, and cut a cross into the surface.

Candied Peel

For after-dinner instead of chocolates. You can use any citrus fruits for this surprisingly delicious and moreish sweet. Grapefruit works particularly well, taking on a translucent quality that's very pretty, particularly if you use different varieties – ruby and yellow.

4 oranges or grapefruits, or a mixture
500g sugar
caster sugar – for coating

Cut the fruit in half and remove the flesh, keeping the peel as intact as possible. Slice the peel into strips 5mm wide. Place in a saucepan and cover with cold water, bringing it to a boil, and allow to cook for 15 minutes. Drain the peel in a colander and discard the water.

Place the peel in the pan and cover with cold water. Bring to the boil and cook for 20 minutes, until the peel is tender.

Meanwhile, put the sugar and 250ml water in a saucepan, heat gently to dissolve the sugar and bring to a boil. Remove the pan from the heat.

Drain the peel again, discarding the water, and put the peel into the pan of syrup. Bring to a bare simmer and allow it to cook, uncovered, for 1 to 1½ hours – there will be very little syrup left and it will all be tremendously sticky.

Line a tray with silicone paper. Using tongs, remove the pieces of peel, one at a time, and place on the silicone paper. Put the tray somewhere cool and airy and allow the peel to dry for a couple of days.

Take a large polythene bag, add a couple of tablespoonsful of sugar, and tip in the peel, giving the bag a good shake to coat the peel evenly with the sugar. The peel will store in an airtight container for several days – if it lasts that long.

Marmalade

This makes enough for us for one year – about 8 jars.

6 Seville oranges
3 lemons
2kg sugar

Wash the fruit well in warm water, using a stiff brush – a nail brush is ideal.

Place a square of muslin in a basin to catch the pips and pith. Cut the oranges and lemons in half and squeeze out the juice, putting the pips in the muslin-lined basin. Slice the fruit – thickly for chunky, or finely, or somewhere in between. Put the fruit, the juice and 2.5 litres water in a large basin.

Tie up the pips, add them to the fruit and allow to soak for 24 hours.

Transfer the contents of the large basin to a preserving or other large pan – but not aluminium – and simmer gently for 2 to 2½ hours. Meanwhile, warm the sugar in a low oven.

When the fruit and water have reduced by half and the peel is tender, stir in the warm sugar to dissolve it then bring to the boil for about 10 minutes or until it says 'jam' on the sugar thermometer – 105°C.

Allow the marmalade to cool in the pan for 20 minutes – this will stop the peel from rising to the top of the jars. Pour into hot, sterilised jars and seal tightly.

Redcurrant Jelly

Invaluable for enriching gravies and stocks, particularly when cooking game dishes. You will need a large measuring jug, and a jelly bag; set it up before you start.

2kg redcurrants, stripped from the stalks using a fork
sugar (see method)

Put the redcurrants into a large stainless or enamelled pan and heat them gently until the juice starts to run. Turn up the heat and simmer the fruit for 30 to 40 minutes, mashing it gently from time to time with the back of a wooden spoon.

Tip the fruit and juice into a jelly bag and allow the juice to drip through, overnight if possible. Resist all urges to help it on its way by pressing.

The next day wash, rinse and dry some glass jars and gently warm in the oven.

Measure the redcurrant juice and allow 500g sugar for every 500ml liquid. Warm the sugar in the oven and gently heat the juice in a large stainless or enamelled pan.

Add the warm sugar to the juice and bring to a boil for 1 minute. Skim the foam from the surface and pour the juice into the hot jars – do all this as fast as possible.

Seal the jars, allow them to cool, and then label them. You will think you will remember what is in the jars, but if you are like us, probably not.

1750
1500
1250
1000
750
500
cca 2000

Vegetable Stock

1kg vegetables – onions, carrots, celery, and leeks, chopped
1.5 litres water
a sprig of parsley
a sprig of thyme
a sprig of lovage
a bay leaf
salt and pepper

Preheat the oven to 220°C (425°F), Gas Mark 7.

Put the vegetables in a roasting tin and bake for about 15 minutes.

Tip the vegetables into a saucepan, add the water, the herbs and some salt and pepper. Cover and simmer for 2 hours, pressing the vegetables from time to time.

Strain the stock into a jug, allow to cool, and then put in the fridge.

This stock will keep for 5 to 7 days if covered and stored in the refrigerator.

Beef Stock

500g shin of beef, finely chopped
500g veal knuckle bones, chopped by your butcher
1 onion, halved
1 carrot, chopped
1 stick of celery, chopped
1.5 litres water
a sprig of parsley
a sprig of thyme
a sprig of lovage
a bay leaf
1 teaspoon salt
a few black peppercorns

Preheat the oven to 220°C (425°F), Gas Mark 7.

Put the beef, bones, onion, carrot and celery in a roasting tin and brown them in the oven for 15 to 20 minutes. Then tip them into a large saucepan.

Deglaze the roasting tin with some of the water and pour it over the beef and vegetables. Add the remaining water, the herbs, salt and peppercorns. Bring to a simmer, skim the scum from the surface, and allow the stock to simmer, covered, for 2 hours.

Strain the stock into a jug, allow it to cool, and then chill until needed.

Remove the fat from the surface of the stock before use.

This stock will keep for 5 to 7 days if covered and stored in the refrigerator.

Chicken Stock

Chicken stock is used in many of the recipes in this book. Well-made stock will form a jelly, but will regain its liquid state on heating.

1kg chicken wings, chopped
1 onion, halved
1 carrot, chopped
1 leek, chopped
25g dried porcini, soaked in a cup of warm water
a sprig of thyme
a bay leaf
50ml white wine
salt and pepper

Preheat the oven to 200°C (400°F), Gas Mark 6.

Put the chicken wings into a baking tin with the onion, carrot and leek. Put the tin in the oven for 8–10 minutes until the chicken and onion have taken on a bit of colour. When they are lightly burnished, tip them into a saucepan together with the dried porcini and their soaking liquid, as well as the thyme and the bay leaf.

Lower the oven temperature to 150°C (300°F), Gas Mark 2. Deglaze the roasting pan with the white wine, then add to the saucepan. Pour in enough water, about 500ml, to barely cover the chicken wings and bring to a simmer. Cover and either keep the pan at a simmer over a low heat, or put into the oven for 40 minutes.

Strain the stock into a jug, pressing down on the wings and vegetables, and allow to cool. Add salt and pepper to taste.

This stock will keep in the fridge for a week, if you boil it up every 2 days.

If you prefer clear stock, add 1 minced chicken breast and 1 egg white per 500ml of stock and bring to a simmer, whisking lightly. When the stock is just below the boil, adjust the heat or move the pan to the side of the stove to let it just shimmer for about 30 minutes. A crust of egg white with the trapped impurities will form on top. You can then remove this with a slotted spoon, revealing the clear broth underneath.

Strain the stock through a sieve lined with muslin to trap any remaining egg white. Leave the stock to cool and then put in the fridge.

Larder Essentials

We're lucky enough to have a large walk-in larder at our house in the country which means we can store quite an amount of provisions. In our flat in London, however, our larder space is limited to an under-counter cupboard with three shelves. We tend to keep the same core items in both homes, although there's not as much need to have things to hand when in town as 24-hour supermarkets and convenience stores on virtually every corner mean that popping out for a few ingredients is relatively easy. Here's a list of what we tend to keep as a matter of course.

Beans – white haricots, split peas, lentils

Chocolate – 70% cocoa solids

Dried fruits – sultanas, currants, apricots, prunes, porcini, morels, chestnuts

Drinks – Tea, coffee, hot chocolate

Flour – Strong white, wholemeal, self-raising, dried yeast, bicarbonate of soda

Jars – olives, peppers, artichokes, tahini, curry paste

Mustard – English, French, pickles, chutney, horseradish, wasabi

Nuts – walnuts, whole and ground almonds, hazelnuts, pine nuts

Oil – olive, grapeseed, walnut

Pasta – lasagne, spaghetti, noodles

Pearl barley

Rice – risotto, basmati, long-grain, pudding

Salt – Maldon

Sauces – anchovy essence, fish sauce, tomato ketchup, mushroom ketchup, Worcestershire sauce, Tabasco sauce, soya sauce

Spices – cumin, cardamom, cinnamon, coriander, nutmeg, mace, juniper berries, cloves, allspice, mixed spice, black and white peppercorns

Spreads – marmalade, apricot jam, marmite

Stock cubes – chicken, beef, Marigold vegetable bouillon

Sugar – demerara, caster, preserving, icing, golden syrup, treacle, honey

Tins – tuna, anchovies, clams, smoked cod roe, tomatoes, passata, coconut milk, Heinz tomato soup, olives, chickpeas

Vinegar – red wine, white wine, cider, sherry, pickling

Paprika
Chili Powder
GOLDEN
HEINZ
TOMATO KETCHUP
Alpen
HEINZ
Tomato soup
BART
les nounours
au chocolat

Equipment

In the immediate post-war years it was impossible to find a decent durable piece of kitchen equipment in the shops – everything was thin, flimsy and tinny; not a heavy-based pan in sight. Then came the great Elizabeth David revolution and we all realised that you need good equipment to cook good food.

Fifty years on and we have a situation that is the complete reverse and is in someway just as much a cause for concern. Every shop selling home-wares is stuffed with kitchen equipment and gadgets, everything you need (and many you don't) readily available. Many kitchen cupboards resemble the overhead lockers on aeroplanes – so full that, if not an actual danger to your life, they certainly are to your sanity.

So if you want to simplify your life and restore your sanity, select the few things that you really need on a day-to-day basis. This way you can find the things you need without them cluttering up the working areas of your kitchen.

Our daily essentials are:

- a really good, thick, wooden chopping board
- two good, sharp knives – one small, one hefty
- a sharpening steel
- wooden spoons and spatulas
- four sizes of heavy-bottomed pans, with one of at least 10 litres
- two cast iron casserole dishes, medium and large
- a large sauté pan
- an omelette pan
- a non-stick milk pan
- two enamelled roasting tins
- a large colander
- a mouli-legumes with two blades, medium and fine
- a four-sided grater
- a conical strainer
- an egg whisk
- a pestle and mortar
- a ladle
- a slotted spoon
- a skimming spoon
- a rolling pin
- a pepper mill and a crock of sea salt
- a pair of weighing scales with metric weights
- plenty of union tea-towels

Of course, like most keen cooks we also have tons of other stuff, mainly stored in cupboards and some of it is used only intermittently. What we suggest is that the decks should be kept clear of extraneous gadgets and rarely-used equipment. Keep your kitchen plain, simple and useful and you will find it more enjoyable to work in.

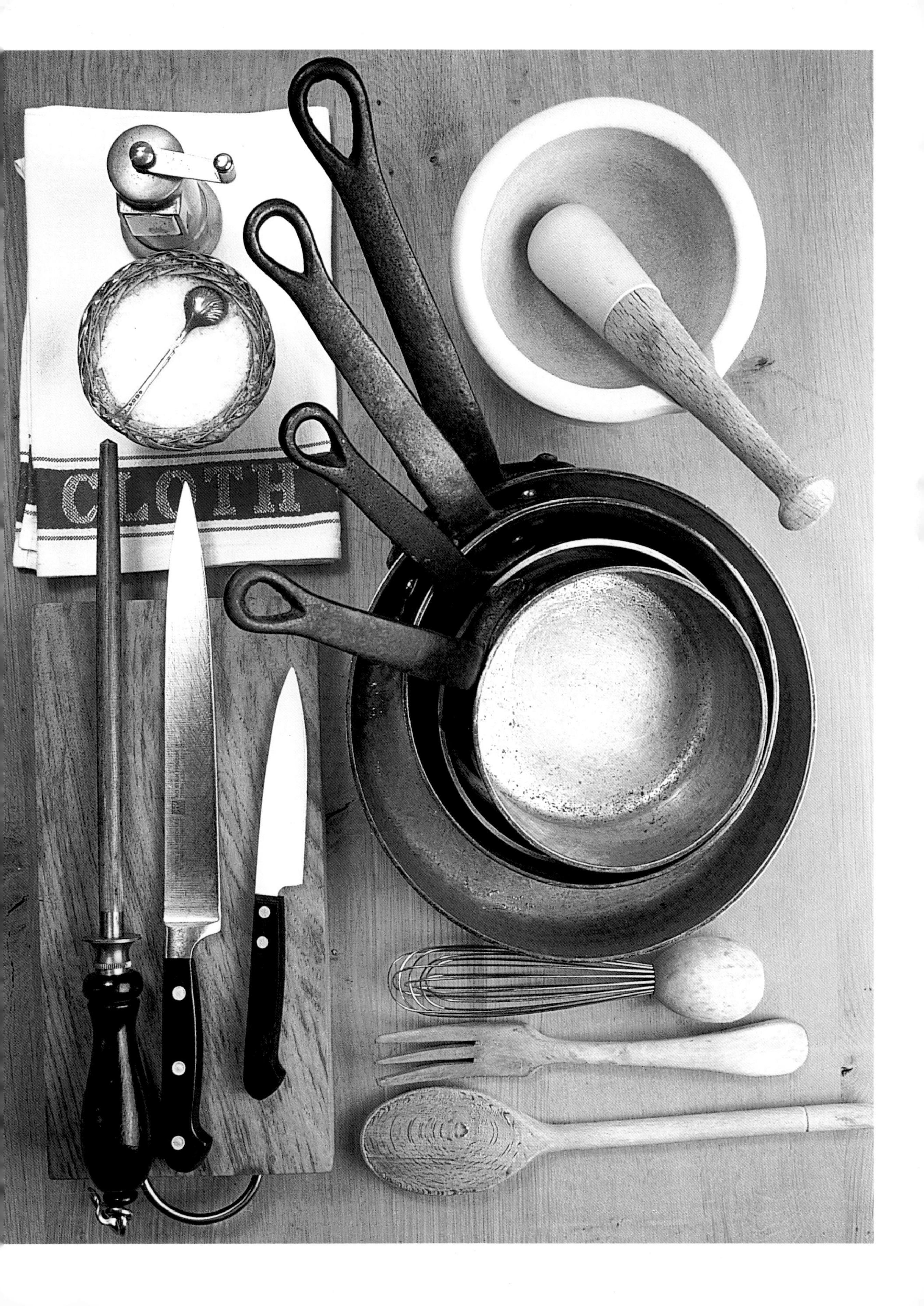
CLOTH

Index

A

B

C

D

E

F

G

H

I

J

K

L

Authors' Acknowledgements:

Jonathan Chidsey – our kitchen gardener. A vital ingredient.

Diane Smith – our housekeeper who keeps the kitchen and the pantry clean and well-organised.

Leslie Harrington – who put her heart and soul into the design and layout.

Georgia Glynn Smith – who photographed everything so beautifully.

No stylist or home economist was necessary as we did the cooking and put the food on the plates as normal.

Knives, pots, pans, plates, bowls and other culinary clutter either came from the Conran Shop or from our own kitchen.